MY PEOPLE IS THE ENEMY

William Stringfellow was educated at Bates College, the London School of Economics, and the Harvard Law School. The author of *A Private and Public Faith* and *Free in Obedience,* he is a frequent contributor both to legal and theological journals. A prominent Episcopal layman, he has been active in the World Council of Churches.

Books by the Same Author

A Private and Public Faith
Instead of Death
Free in Obedience

MY PEOPLE
IS THE ENEMY

AN AUTOBIOGRAPHICAL POLEMIC
BY WILLIAM STRINGFELLOW

ANCHOR BOOKS
DOUBLEDAY & COMPANY, INC.
GARDEN CITY, NEW YORK

For Jeanne and James Breeden

My People Is the Enemy was originally published by
Holt, Rinehart and Winston, Inc., in 1964.
The Anchor Books edition is published by
arrangement with Holt, Rinehart and Winston, Inc.
Anchor Books edition 1966.

Behold, he is coming with the clouds, and every eye will see him, every one who pierced him; and all tribes of the earth will wail on account of him. Even so. Amen.

The Revelation to John 1:7

Chapter One
INITIATION

The stairway smelled of piss.

The smells inside the tenement—number 18, 342 East 100th Street, Manhattan—were somewhat more ambiguous. They were a suffocating mixture of rotting food, rancid mattresses, dead rodents, dirt, and the stale odors of human life.

This was to be home. It had been home before: for a family of eight—five kids, three adults. Some of their belongings had been left behind. Some of their life had, too.

The place, altogether, was about 25 × 12 feet, with a wall separating the kitchen section from the rest. In the kitchen was a bathtub, a tiny, rusty sink, a refrigerator that didn't work, and an ancient gas range. In one corner was a toilet with a bowl without a seat. Water dripped perpetually from the box above the bowl. The other room was filled with beds: two double-decker military cots, and a big ugly convertible sofa. There wasn't room for anything else. The walls and ceilings were mostly holes and patches and peeling paint, sheltering legions of cockroaches.

This was to be my home.

I wondered, for a moment, why.

Then I remembered that this is the sort of place in which most people live, in most of the world, for most of the time. This or something worse.

Then I was home.

It was to Harlem that I came from the Harvard Law School.

I came to Harlem to live, to work there as a lawyer, to take some part in the politics of the neighborhood, to be a layman in the Church there.

It is now seven years later.

In what I relate about Harlem, I do not wish to indulge in horror stories, though that would be easy enough to do. Even less do I wish to be analytical—to recite the statistics of poverty or to speculate about the coincidence of poverty with racial segregation or to probe the causes of poverty and racism in America or to venture speculations about how any of the issues of poverty and racism may be somehow resolved. I am by no means sure that in this world, such issues can be resolved.

Be cautioned that in what follows I am only a witness, testifying, as accurately as I am able, to what I myself have seen and heard during the time I lived and worked in Harlem.

I am an Anglo-Saxon white man, not a Negro nor a Puerto Rican, and I do not pretend in any sense to speak for the Negroes or the Puerto Ricans of Harlem. They don't need white men to speak for them—they speak for themselves with ample clarity and admirable passion.

I try here only to relate what I see happening in Harlem and what I hear Harlem saying nowadays.

Only that—and a word or two about the terrible premonition I suffer about what lies ahead for all Americans in the harsh days which come upon the nation in the crisis of racism and poverty in the cities of the land.

Only that—and some word, too, about the theological

significance of the hostility between the rich and the poor, and the alienation between the races, and how reconciliation is wrought.

In other words, I seek here only to describe the milieu of my own life and work during the years I have been in Harlem and, from that, to emphasize the moral ambiguity of social policy and legislation which intend to cope with slum housing and delinquency and deteriorated schools and racial discrimination and narcotics traffic and public welfare and unemployability and all the rest which characterize the internal life of the urban ghettos.

The Vulnerability of the Poor

I lived in the section called East Harlem—on 100th Street, between First and Second Avenues—on the block which *The New York Times* calls the "worst" in the city. The external appearance of the neighborhood there is radically different from Northampton, Massachusetts, where I was raised, or from Cambridge, where I studied law, but it is also different from most other sections of New York City. In the city, affluence, inflation, luxury, and power are only a few blocks away, but in Harlem, there is squalor, depression, poverty, and frustration. Harlem is largely neglected by and segregated from the rest of the city. Outside are air purifiers, private toilets, hi-fi, gourmet food, imported cars, and the extra-dry martini; inside Harlem are the smells of sweat and waste, bathtubs in the kitchens, antiquated direct current, predatory vermin, second-hand clothes, and a million empty beer cans in the gutters. Outside the ghetto are secure jobs, some chance for education, and even space to play; inside, there is chronic unemployment, much illiteracy, and the numbers game. Outside, people have recourse to psychotherapy, positive thinking, and Carte Blanche;

inside, people have narcotics, the pawn shop, and cadres of social workers. In Harlem, Park Avenue becomes a railroad track.

On the western side of that railroad track, some of the slums have been demolished and some of the people are middle class and some are even *nouveaux riches,* but in East Harlem little has really changed from the time that I first moved there; and the overwhelming reality for most of those who live in Harlem on both sides of the track is poverty.

Poverty means not just density of population or large families or dilapidated housing or infestation of vermin or the absence of privacy or obsolescent sanitation or low income or unemployability or retarded education or indifferent politicians or the congestion of the streets—it is all of these tangled up in the life of each person. At least that is the way I was exposed to poverty every day I lived in Harlem.

The social engineers are beguiled when they suppose that any of these issues can be isolated from the rest, or that, in dealing with any of them, the particularity of the situation of each person can be minimized or ignored.

Poverty—the poverty that I beheld in my clients and neighbors—is an essentially personal burden—just as, the Psalms remind us, riches are also. Poverty was my very first client in Harlem—a father whose child died from being attacked by a rat. Poverty is a widow on welfare whose landlord cuts the heat, knowing that the winter will end before a complaint is processed. Poverty is a drug addict who steals from his own family or pawns the jacket off his back to get another "fix." Poverty is being evicted from a housing project because the project manager determines that the family is "undesirable." Poverty is a Puerto Rican shopkeeper whose store is stoned when he tries to relocate south of the 96th Street boundary of East Harlem. Poverty is an adolescent with a tested I.Q. of

130 who cannot read or write the English languge well enough to get other than the most menial jobs. Poverty is the pay-off to a building inspector not to report violations of the building code. Poverty is a young couple who marry because that is the only way to get out of the tenements and into a project, and whose marriage fails, and who have neither the grounds for a divorce in New York nor the price for a divorce in another jurisdiction. Poverty is being awakened in the middle of the night by a welfare investigator who demands to search your apartment to be sure you are not cheating the taxpayers. Poverty is the incapacity to complain against the landlord because you can't afford to take a day off from your job or from minding the family to go to court. Poverty is a kid who wants to be adopted to escape from the slums but whom no one wants. Poverty is a boy whose father has thrown him out, a boy who needs a place to stay. Poverty is living in darkness after the electric current has been turned off as a fire hazard, and waiting for six or seven days until someone is sent to repair the obsolete wiring.

Poverty is the enormous burden of waiting—waiting for hours for a doctor to examine a sick child at the hospital clinic, waiting for an interview with a social worker, waiting at the employment office, waiting in line for what the government ironically calls "surplus" food, waiting for everything, everywhere you go.

Poverty is vulnerability to death in its crudest forms. Poverty is the relentless daily attrition of contending with the most primitive concerns of human existence: food and cleanliness and clothes and heat and housing and rest and play and work.

The Anatomy of Poverty

Perhaps the most obvious contrast between New York's Harlem and the outer city is its acute density of population. In the East Harlem section alone—an area roughly equivalent to one square mile—live about two hundred thousand people. Nobody is really certain of the number; apparently no one has ever taken a full census. An old man in the neighborhood can recollect no census taker ever bothering to canvass his block. So far as the outer city is concerned, though the poor be many, they are anonymous. In any case, population density is very great in Harlem and it is greatest in East Harlem. In my view, social workers spend too much time with statistics, but they do know their statistics, and one social worker I know computes that if the entire population of the United States—190,000,000 people—lived in as severe proximity as people in fact do live in East Harlem, the whole population could be housed in the five boroughs of New York City.

I do not have the imagination to visualize such computations. But I do see the block where I myself lived. There, about four thousand people—an entire village—inhabit twenty-seven crumbling tenement buildings. And I know that eight people had occupied my tiny apartment. When that many people live in that little space, population density is very existential: it means someone is always in the toilet, the sink is generally in use, the stove is going most of the time—when not to cook, then to heat the house —and the beds have to be used in shifts.

It means more than that. When so many people live so close together, even though they're your own family, there is really no such thing as private property. Even if you somehow acquire some item of personal property— clothing or athletic equipment or the like—there's no place to put it where you can be sure no one else will touch it or wear it or borrow it or use it or steal it or trespass it in one way or another.

And it means more important things than that—it means that there is no possibility of privacy. If the parents of such a family have the ordinary relationships of marriage, there is no place for them to have intercourse out of the sight of their children. If, as happens at least as often among poor people as among rich, the husband or the wife or both are unfaithful to their marriage and have other sexual partners, there is nowhere they can be private, and so the children see that too. It is said that loneliness is a profound problem of people in American society, but it is also debilitating to a person to have no place and no opportunity to be alone. Especially for adolescents, the absence of privacy is distressing. A kid in East Harlem grows up without the chance to be alone. He can never do anything without being watched; he cannot have the secret and private life of his own that every child needs.

Life amidst such congestion means for adults that there is no room in which to take leisure in the home, or to entertain a guest; and for children, there is no place to play indoors. The street, therefore, becomes more a locus of life than the tenements, notably in hot weather when the tenements steam and stink. There is some escape in the street. For play there are puddles and rubbish and alleys to roam and stickball and checkers and blackjack and craps, and sometimes a cockfight. There are jukeboxes in the candy stores, so there is dancing in the street. There is vicarious joy in the esoteric religious sects in storefronts on the street. There are places to sit—fire escapes and car fenders and curbstones. In short, there is society in the street among neighbors from the block.

But the street is also a precarious, primitive society: it is the locale of bookies and the numbers racket, of pimps and dope pushers and pay-offs and other parasites of poverty. The street is violent: three times I have witnessed shootings there. For some, the street means the threat of raids from rival gangs; for addicts, there is the risk of being fingered by a stooge purchasing his own immunity from arrest; for most, there is the fear of harassment by the police who seem somehow like an occupation army. The street is a jungle.

The street is a society, but also a jungle: a place to play and a place to fight. That applies particularly to adolescents who grow up in the slums of Harlem. To be sure, in the past few years there have been some improvements in the facilities available within the neighborhood for kids to play—playgrounds and gymnasiums and the like—off the street. But these facilities are nowhere near adequate for the numbers of children and youth in the neighborhood. When I was a boy I could play ball every afternoon, if I wanted to, and all day Saturday and *almost* all day Sunday; and in the summers there were a hundred places in which to roam, and there were places to swim and hike, and so on. That is not the case at all for multitudes of urban adolescents, for whom the street remains virtually the only place for play.

There is too little space to play and there are too few things to play with. One of the favorite playthings and pieces of athletic equipment available in the streets is the empty beer can. The children invent all kinds of toys and games, using discarded beer cans.

So a child grows up in Harlem, and reaches the time when, as a teen-ager, his physical, emotional, psychic, and intellectual capabilities erupt all at once—when he arrives at a peak of his energies and has a great need to find out what he can do with his own body and mind. Play is an important, if not the main, means of his self-discovery, but in such a neighborhood, for all too many, there is no place to play.

The frustration of such confinement for an adolescent is obvious. One of the compensations for the absence of opportunity for play in Harlem is gang society.

Much—I am inclined to think too much—has been written and said about the adolescent gangs in the city, and their rumbles and wars and violence and antisocial behavior. I will say only this much here:

The rumble, the gang war, as far as I can discern, functions for these kids as a highly concentrated, compensatory form of play. For a boy who is deprived of playing football every afternoon, the rumble becomes, whatever else it may also represent, a very dramatic, very exciting, very compressed game. In perhaps as little as twenty minutes it is over, but in that time a boy makes up for months and months of physical, intellectual, emotional, and psychic frustration, stored up from the lack of opportunity to play.

Notice another fact which is often overlooked about gang society in city slums. Many adolescents in Harlem and similar neighborhoods come from so-called broken homes. In American society, that, of course, is by no means an issue peculiar to poor people or people who have suffered racial discrimination. There is ample evidence of profligate delinquency and antisocial protest among privileged youngsters, and there is certainly a high incidence of divorce, marital infidelity, absentee parents, and the like in the families in which privileged youths are raised. Whatever the case may be in Westchester, in Harlem many youngsters grow up largely on their own because of the size of the families and the crowdedness of the homes; and many grow up without the presence, security, example, guidance, or love of a father. Sometimes the child is illegitimate and the father has deserted the mother and child; sometimes there are desertions, though there has been a legal marriage; sometimes the father is conscientious and supports the family, but in order to do so must be absent most of the time and, when he returns to the tenement, needs to rest for the next day's work and has little time for his children. Often there are so many children that each one receives scant attention. And so, for all practical purposes, many children grow up in Harlem without ever really having known a father; in these circumstances, particularly for boys, the gang becomes a substitute for the father. The essential responsibility of a father to his children, and perhaps especially to his sons, is to show them how to survive in this world in the specific circumstances in which they happen to live. In gang society the older boys teach the younger ones how to survive—how to survive in the jungle of the street —and thus, for many boys, the gang replaces the absentee father.

I do not know too much at first hand about the internal life of the public schools in Harlem, and so make no generalizations, partly because what I do know is so horrendous. One hopes there is another side to the story. A symbol in my own recollection about the Harlem schools is the episode a couple of years ago involving a public school which was in particularly decrepit condition. The parents of students and some of the teachers had long been complaining to the educational administration and to their political representatives about the conditions in the building. A newspaper took up their complaints and ran some articles exposing the situation. Finally, and only after months of pressure, the Mayor of New York, a man of extravagant apathy, decided to visit the premises to see what they were like. This is typical of the mentality which rules the political administration of New York—that is, no issue or problem or crisis is acted upon until it becomes so notorious that some sort of action is a political and public necessity. There is little evidence that the Mayor seriously cares about such matters until his own public self-interest becomes in some fashion involved. And even then the "action" taken to appease the press and public is more often than not a gesture, like the appointment of a Mayor's Committee to investigate, or a visit from the Mayor to "find out for himself what's going on" and a promise that he will remedy whatever may be amiss. In

this case the Mayor elected the latter course of "action."
He arranged to visit the school in question, inspect the
premises, and speak to the students, teachers, and parents assembled for his visitation. The day came and the
Mayor, accompanied by a retinue of photographers and
reporters, was about to mount the platform when—by
what I am disposed to consider an act of God—a huge
rat ran across the stage. The incident was duly reported
in all the newspapers and, of course, the school had to be
closed, at least until the rats had been exterminated. This
was done. The school reopened a couple of weeks later,
after, it is said, the exterminator carted off more than two
hundred rat carcasses. Then the students and teachers returned. But they had to be evacuated again promptly. So
many more rats, killed by the extermination, lay hidden
and rotting in the walls that the building was still unin-
habitable. Subsequently, some repairs have been made in
the building, but it is still not scheduled to be replaced as
a public school for several more years.

Not all schools in Harlem are like this one. The point is
—far too many of them are. Even one such school is too
many. How it is to be expected that children can be educated in conditions such as prevail in some Harlem schools
is a question that is answered by parents of students and
the students themselves who attend such schools in the
only way that can possibly make sense to them: *Nobody
cares whether they receive an education or not.*

And many do not receive any education worthy of the
name, though they complete their full terms in school. For
example, take a boy from Harlem who was charged with
perpetual truancy during the last two years he was enrolled
in high school, and whom I represented in his difficulties
with the school authorities. During the time Bob was in
trouble, I arranged to have him take a battery of written
and oral tests at a private educational rehabilitation
agency in the city. These tests established that though he

had great difficulty with reading and writing, though he was functionally almost illiterate in the English language, he was of superior intelligence. It was also established that physically and psychologically he was in good health, and that his attitudes toward learning and work were affirmative—he wanted to learn so that he could get a job. Yet, somehow, he had gone through years in the Harlem public schools without mastering the most elementary occupational skill required in urban society—language. Apparently, the reason he began being truant was that he became bored with the tedium of school and discouraged about the prospect of learning much of anything useful in school. He quit school, but he did not give up; he tried to find a job. Of course, he could not, because he lacked a school certificate for work and could not legally be employed; and, because of his limited language skills, he encountered great difficulties in completing applications for employment. He did find a few odd jobs—moving furniture and running errands—menial jobs where the employer was willing to take him on part time, for little pay, on the side, without a work certificate; but these were hardly situations in which he could learn anything, except to learn that he was not really wanted and—in spite of his intelligence—apparently not needed in this society. After a long period of truancy, he was picked up by the school authorities. Even that was a discouragement to him—that he could skip school for months and no one seemed to care enough to find out where he was or why he wasn't in school. At a conference on his case with a school official, in my presence, it was explained to Bob that if he didn't want to go back to school, that was his business; but the school system had to maintain a record of his school attendance until such time, then about four months off, that he could legally quit school. So Bob was placed in what is called a "continuation" school, a special facility with a reduced class schedule where he could be enrolled in order nominally to complete his public-school education. Absurdly, for a boy who, first of all, needed some language training, he was assigned to a course in typing. After he had gone for a few days to this school, he told me that he was having difficulty with the typing lessons because he could not spell and because the manual in use was sometimes hard for him to read and understand. However, he had figured out how to make repairs on the typewriter when the machine he used broke down, and he had spent much of his time repairing other machines the class was using. Shortly after that, he told the instructor that this was a waste of time for him—at least on the outside he might find a few part-time jobs—and he and the instructor agreed that he would no longer have to attend the classes, provided he was recorded as in attendance, and provided that he showed up now and then for an interview concerning his "progress" in continuation school, about which occasional records had to be kept in the school system. Bob went along with this pretense and was in due course "discharged" from continuation school, more certain than ever before that nobody seriously cares, in the schools of New York, whether he is in school, much less whether he learns or does anything there, so long as the records are kept straight and so long as the instructors and administrators are thereby protected. Who is to say that he should think any differently? And who knows how many other thousands of Bobs there are, and have been, over the years?

Bob's experience is not related, let it be emphasized, in order to imply that it is the only side of the story in Harlem's schools; rather, it is to say that his is not an isolated nor a particularly exceptional case. Such cases occur far too often to far too many kids, and have occurred for far too many years. Let it be said, too, that there are a great many competent, concerned, and dedicated teachers and administrators in Harlem's schools; but many of them are as much victims of the same conditions from which Bob suffered and still suffers.

Where the schools are grossly overcrowded, the teacher and administrator are inhibited from educating the children by having to be preoccupied with discipline. Where the facilities are outmoded and crumbling, as in one school where there are toilet facilities in only one room, so that boys and girls can use them only at the times designated for their sex, it is difficult for either teachers or students to concentrate on studies. Where uncertified, less experienced substitute teachers are employed and placed in schools which are most congested and overenrolled, and where the students come from overcrowded streets and tenements—and sometimes from disrupted and difficult homes and families—it may be virtually impossible either to teach or to learn. Where most of the teachers are commuters, living in quite different circumstances in most respects from the students and their parents, there is a great barrier to the empathy between teacher and student and parent that is so essential to education. Where children are aware, along with their parents, that they are segregated from the rest of the city, even in their schools, and see that their schools are far inferior to the schools provided for the rest of society, they are apt to conclude, as Bob has, that they are not welcome or wanted in American society.

Kids like Bob go to school and receive nothing there which fits them for life and work in the city. If the young person is conscientious, as Bob was for a while, he tramps the streets and tries and tries and tries to get a job. But because he is Negro or Puerto Rican, because of his functional illiteracy, because his clothes may not be as presentable as other applicants', because he's not a member of a particular union and finds that he can't get into it when he applies, he ends up, if he's lucky, with some part-time, short-term, marginal, menial job.

You will find them in jobs like those which Bob has from time to time—errand boys and messengers, cleaning workers in office buildings, kitchen help in hotels and restaurants, janitors and shoeshiners. Sometimes you will find them in somewhat more skilled, or status, jobs—as elevator operators or hospital orderlies or office help or doormen. You will find them—most of them who still have jobs—in exactly the jobs most threatened by automation. I am told that there are nearly a quarter of a million elevator operators in this country, chiefly in the cities, who are now certain of imminently losing their jobs because of automation. Many of these people are middle aged, many are Negroes, many are people with families to support, many have no other recognized skill at all. Including their families, upwards of a million people will be directly affected by the automation of elevators. Such people in such jobs, now so rapidly being eliminated from the economy, will become not only unemployed but unemployable in a very short time. Yet very little has yet been undertaken either publicly or privately, by government, business, or the unions to accommodate this adjustment.

The impending elimination of jobs, due to automation, has tended to accentuate racial discrimination in employment. New York Negroes, for instance, in part prompted by the acceleration in automation and the increase in unemployment and unemployability, have demonstrated against discrimination in the building and construction trades in the city—a field, given the planned obsolescence and recurring inflation in commercial and public construction, which is apt to survive automation for some time. After nearly a year of demonstrations involving hundreds of persons, many of whom were arrested, after thousands of applicants for jobs in these trades, only a handful of Negroes have been hired. In the plumbing trade it is the same story. Plumbing is likely to outlast automation; indeed, if somehow this trade is automated, the human race might as well finally surrender to the machine, for we will have been humiliatingly defeated! Yet this trade is closed to all but a few Negroes.

In places like Oxford, Mississippi, there is token integration. That is about all there is in New York, too.

One attempt to meet not only the problem of automation, but also of school dropouts (like Bob), has been launched recently by the government, in collaboration with certain private agencies in New York. It is the so-called Mobilization for Youth. Thirteen million dollars have been made available for this "pilot" project, directed at training and retraining young people for jobs. One interesting sidelight about this program is that the area selected for the experiment (if anything costing thirteen million dollars can be called an experiment) is a section of the Lower East Side. It is a difficult and depressed section of the city, but it is by no means the most difficult or the most depressed section of the city. But the point is that the experiment has been set up under conditions more favorable to its "success" than if it had been attempted in other areas of the city. Not long ago, some of the youth of that neighborhood began picketing the headquarters of Mobilization, alleging in their placards that the enterprise had resulted chiefly in providing jobs for social workers rather than for them, though their signs put it in a more pithy way. Not long after the picketing incident, I had occasion to confer with some of those on the staff of Mobilization and to inquire what had really happened since the program had been initiated, with a good deal of political fanfare, several months earlier. It was reported to me that in the initial six or seven months of the program, roughly twice as many people had been employed to staff Mobilizaton for Youth as young people had been placed in jobs or training situations. I favor joining the kids on the picket line!

Of those from the neighborhood who do have jobs, most have marginal jobs, which are the first to be cut back when the economy contracts. Both illiteracy and the lack of opportunity for education and training for jobs contribute to this, and automation greatly aggravates this situation and portends an even greater unemployment as more and more marginal jobs are eliminated in the city economy. Racial discrimination in trades that are apt to survive automation is by no means operative only in the building and construction fields. There are very few openings for Negroes or Puerto Ricans, for instance, in the banks, especially as tellers or in other positions requiring direct contact with the public. Except in Harlem itself, it is very hard to find a Negro bartender or news dealer in the city; and even within Harlem, it is only very recently that some of the larger retail stores have begun to hire Negroes. In such circumstances, a talented and conscientious worker is often forced to move from one menial and marginal job to another and thus compile such an erratic record of part-time and short-term jobs that potential employers are disinclined to hire him. Moreover, his personal capabilities and potential occupational skills never have a chance to be concentrated and to mature, which frustrates any actual freedom to choose a trade.

Meanwhile, unemployment compensation is an aid only to those who have had a minimum regularity in work during the year; and welfare assistance in New York City depends very much on who the investigator is and whether or not a given case fits the categories invented by the sociologists. The classifications in public welfare can sometimes be grotesquely oblivious to actual human need.

Where there is employment in a family, the chances are that for everyone with a job, there are one or two others able and old enough to work who are unemployed. One wage often supports six or eight or more people. At the same time, the requirements which entitle a family to public housing actually encourage people who might go to work not to do so. Gross family income determines qualification for public housing, and employable members of a family may remain idle or fraudulently conceal jobs in order that the family will not be dispossessed of a project apartment and be forced to move back to a slum tenement.

Meanwhile, the fiction is maintained that rent control protects the poor in the slums from high rents. The fact is that in many, many cases, the provisions of the law which permit automatic increases each time the tenancy changes mean that some slum tenements—similar to the tiny one that I lived in—will have a rent of ninety or a hundred dollars a month, or even higher, according to how many changes of tenancy there have been since the law originated at the beginning of the Second World War. Exorbitant rents for slum dwellings force some families to double up with relatives and share the same premises.

At the same time, recourse to the Rent Commission for redress of grievances against landlords who charge illegal rents is for many a discouraging experience. Most tenants cannot afford counsel for such a proceeding and thus are confronted by the landlord's lawyer and a hearing officer without the opportunity to be fully informed about their rights. Moreover, testimony is taken in such proceedings without an oath, which is an invitation to the landlord to lie with impunity. There are enough instances of bribery to convince many tenants that it is a waste of time to complain against a landlord. In the course of some of the cases before the Rent Commission which I have handled, I became acquainted with a certain real estate man who was extraordinarily knowledgeable about which hearing officers could be bought. After learning the identity of an officer assigned to one of my cases, I would sometimes consult this man in order to ascertain whether the officer in question was one who accepted such gratuities—not, I might add, in order to offer him a bribe, but to try to determine whether or not he might have been bought by the landlord, so that I could then attempt to have the case reassigned to another officer.

It ought to be kept in mind, by the way, that not all slum landlords are greedy, greasy, wicked men, reaping huge profits—as much, sometimes, as twenty-five per cent—from the misery of the poor. Some of the heaviest investors are institutions—insurance companies, universities, unions, and, alas, churches. And I have had cases where the landlord turned out to be clergymen.

Even where the rents are cheap, the buildings are old and crowded, repairs are made infrequently and are predictably ineffectual. Sanitation facilities are obsolete and overtaxed, wiring is defective and outmoded, health and building inspectors—even waiving the question of corruption—are usually unavailable and overworked; the landlords are generally absentees and inaccessible except for the collection of the rents and profits; the tenants are ignorant of their rights and mostly too poor to enforce them. Tenants who do try to enforce their rights learn that after taking a day off from work to go to court, the case will be adjourned, and this will be repeated, so that the tenant cannot afford the economic attrition of following up his complaint, especially when, in the end, the landlord gets off with a nominal fine, and the condition complained of remains uncorrected.

Priority for housing redevelopment in Harlem has been consistently lower than that of less-blighted sections of New York City, but, apart from that, the projects which have been constructed caused the remaining slums to become more congested than ever. Those whom the housing authorities determine to be "undesirable" may not be admitted to project tenancies—and the "undesirables"—those

with the largest families, or those who have had trouble
with the law, or those who are unemployed and thus are
bad rent risks, those addicted to narcotics, those whose
kids are associated with "antisocial" gangs—are those who
most need to move out of the slums.

At the same time, housing redevelopment dispossesses
those who have lived in the tenements on the site, and
often replaces them with people from other parts of the
city, rather than actually providing new housing for the
dispossessed. For many of those evicted to make way for
the new housing, the only place to move is to the remaining slum tenements, which thereby become even more
congested. The classic example of this, in my observation,
was the development through private investment with
public subsidy of a co-operative apartment project in
Harlem. The theory was that the neighborhood would be
improved if such a project were built and attracted into
the neighborhood "a more stable element." Several blocks
of tenements were demolished and the tenants were forced
to move elsewhere. The project was completed after
about three years of construction. Apartments were offered
for sale at a comparatively low purchase price and main-
tenance rate. For months now, the project has remained
substantially underoccupied because so few families from
the neighborhood, including those who had been dispossessed, could afford even these relatively low costs, and
because "the more stable element" elsewhere in the city
was reluctant to move into this virtual "island," sur-
rounded as it is by a sea of slums.

More and more space in other parts of the city—outside the ghetto—is being devoted to building and recon-
structing housing which is simply too expensive for those
who live in the ghetto to afford, even if *de facto* segregation did not exist. In fact, the premium rents for such new
or renovated housing is the chief form of *de facto* segregation in the outer city. The net result, in any case, is that in

the outer city, more and more space is allotted to fewer
and fewer people, while in the inner city, less and less
space is available to more and more people.

There have been some who have come forward to com-
bat all of this—the perpetuation of slums as profitable
investments, along with all the accompanying issues of
pay-offs, the collapse of education, discrimination in employment, and the vices of the street. Father James Gusweller is one of these, though by no means the only one.
He became so incensed with the conditions in which the
people on his block lived that he exposed their plight in
the newspapers, and launched, a few years back, a cru-
sade to remedy these conditions. At the request of the
Episcopal Bishop of New York, I served as Father Gusweller's counsel. After months and months of exposure
and complaint under the glare of sustained publicity by
the newspapers, the city launched a "crash" program to
clean up this block. Today, if you visit that block you will
find that it has significantly improved over what it was
when Father Gusweller began his effort. But go then to
the very next block and you will find all of the same things
which he exposed still persistent there. Aside from my
genuine admiration for Father Gusweller, I am mainly
impressed with the enormity of the passion and persever-
ance which he and the people of his congregation and
others had to sustain and suffer in order to achieve such a
modest change. I am mostly impressed with the massive
indifference of the political authorities to conditions of
which they were chargeable with knowledge long before
Father Gusweller and the publicity which, through him,
these conditions were given. Or to put it a bit differently,
not every block in the slums is so fortunate as to have a
Gusweller to intercede. And yet apart from intercessions
such as his, there is little evidence that the political administration of the city will make any effort to relieve the
indignities which the people of the slums endure. That

in itself indeed may be the greatest indignity which the people of the slums bear: Nobody in the city's political administration, and few others, except an occasional Gusweller, seems to know about them or to care for them.

It is a very dehumanizing and threatening experience to live in the slums. I remember, as vividly as I remember anything, that first day when I went to East 100th Street in Harlem. I had been there one or two times before, to visit some of the clergy who lived and worked in the East Harlem Protestant Parish, and I initially moved to the neighborhood at the suggestion of George Todd, a young Presbyterian minister with the parish, a friend of mine since the days when we had been colleagues in the student Christian movement. Todd had said that often they dealt with situations in which a lawyer was needed, but they had difficulty securing legal help, although there were two or three attorneys in the city who gave all the help they could to the parish. So I agreed to come to Harlem and to be associated with the parish as a lawyer, serving people from the neighborhood in need of legal assistance. The parish had arranged for me to move into the tenement on 100th Street, which, as one of the clergy put it as he handed me the keys to the place, was typical of the housing of the neighborhood. It was Labor Day, 1956, when I came to the city, and I had checked my luggage at Grand Central Station before going uptown to see my new home. I had taken one precaution for my first inspection of the premises—I had a DDT bomb (of the sort that was used in the Army), which I had picked up at a military surplus store. I entered the apartment and looked around. I found a dead mouse in the toilet, which I disposed of. I opened a window, so as not to DDT myself, and then I released the bomb. I sat down on something for a moment to see what would happen. From everywhere—from every crack and corner, from the ceiling and walls and from underneath the linoleum, from out of the refrigerator and the stove, from in back of the sink and under the bathtub, from every place—came swarms of creeping, crawling vermin. I shuddered. I remember saying out loud to myself, "Stringfellow, you will never know here whether you have become an alcoholic." Who could tell, in such a place, whether or not he is having delirium tremens?

I left the place, went downtown, had a drink, checked into a hotel, and spent the night there.

The next day, as it happened, I was to have lunch with Bishop James Pike, who was at that time still the Dean of the Cathedral of St. John the Divine in New York. I told him, though it was perhaps not the most suitable subject for mealtime conversation, about the episode I have just related here. And he replied, "Oh, cheer up! We have cockroaches at the high altar in the Cathedral!"

With that comfort, I returned to East 100th Street and began to sweep up the vermin that had been killed by the DDT. That night I slept in my new home.

In the days that immediately followed, I spent a lot of time just trying to make my new household habitable. I remember using over thirty pounds of putty just to seal the spaces between the floor and the walls, and making innumerable other repairs in the apartment. My first few months in East Harlem made me a household handyman, with experience in wiring, plastering, elementary carpentry, and other such skills. It was during those days, when I was trying to make a place to live in, against the odds which prevail in such a building, that I began to realize and appreciate the extremity of the attrition which they suffer whose daily life is in such apartments, in such tenements, in such neighborhoods—they who, what with families and all, had every day much more to contend with than I did. I remember my exhaustion from trying to maintain my own one life there. How much more exacting and costly it must be for a parent of a family of five or six children, and particularly one who did not have the option, as I did, to return to the outer city.

Finally, a place to live was wrought, though I was promptly and aptly reminded that for me to make a place to live in, in the midst of the Harlem slums, still meant something quite different from what it would be for someone—a Negro or a Puerto Rican—indigenous to these same slums. One symbol of that, in my own experience, is contained in a conversation I had with a Negro from the neighborhood whom I had come to know and whom I bumped into on the street one morning. He stopped me and suggested that we have a cup of coffee, which we did. During the conversation he mentioned that he had noticed that I shined my shoes every day—a custom in which I had been indoctrinated five years before while serving with the Second Armored Division in Germany. He said he knew that this represented the continuation, in my new life in Harlem, of the life that I had formerly lived; and he added that he was glad of it, because it meant that I had remained myself and had not contrived to change, just because I had moved into a different environment. In order, in other words, as I heard him, to be a person in Harlem, in order that my life and work there should have integrity, I had to be and to remain whoever I had become as a person before coming there. To be accepted by others, a man must first of all know himself and accept himself and be himself wherever he happens to be. In that way, others are also freed to be themselves.

To come to Harlem involved, thus, no renunciation of my own past or of any part of it. There was no occasion in Harlem to repudiate anything in my own history and heritage as a white Anglo-Saxon Protestant, nor to seek to identify with the people of Harlem, either by attempting to imitate any of them or by urging any of them to imitate me. What was necessary was just to be myself. I had learned something about that long before moving to

Harlem. I learned it, as I suppose others have, in the military service. I recall feeling somewhat resentful about military service when I first entered the Army after college. It seemed an interruption in my education and career, not wholly a waste of time, given the conditions in the world then, but a sort of void which would not further me personally in any significant way. Most other guys felt about the same, I think. I soon discovered that I was dead wrong. I found that I could be, and was, fulfilled as a person just as much in the service as in school or work—that where I happen to be and what I happen to be doing does not determine the issue of who I am as a human being, or how my own person may be expressed and fulfilled. I learned the meaning of vocation in the Army. It was an emancipating discovery, for then it became possible to go anywhere and to do any sort of work —in full knowledge of my own identity and integrity.

So, moving to Harlem, for all its differences in empirical ways from other places where I had lived, was really an easy thing to do. And as my friend pointed out, when he noticed that my shoes were shined, coming to Harlem did not mean desertion of my past; it meant bringing it with me into a new situation. There was no need for any psychological disassociation, nor was there any practical disassociation, either. I am a lawyer, and I continued, all the years I was in Harlem, to remain in contact with colleagues in the downtown law firms and in the law schools in New York and elsewhere. I found my own practice of the law in Harlem intellectually provocative, and therefore I continued to write and speak about some of the issues of the law and the philosophy of the law with faculty and students from the law schools and with fellow lawyers. I am an Episcopalian, and I had long been active in the affairs of the Episcopal Church. This continued during the time in Harlem, in participation in the congregation to which I belonged and in many other ways as well.

I am a white man, and to live in Harlem did not mean that I need be separated from white society. In fact, as I reflect upon it, there was the marvelous luxury, in living and working in Harlem, of somehow being free and able to transcend a lot of barriers that otherwise separate men from each other. In the course of a day I crossed a good many boundaries: Perhaps I would be in court in the morning with an addict or a kid from one of the gangs, then have lunch with a law professor at Columbia or N.Y.U., interview clients back at 100th Street during the afternoon, have a drink with some of Harlem's community leaders at Frank's Chop House on 125th Street, have dinner with clergy friends or with fellow parishioners at a midtown restaurant, stop for a bull session with some of the law students or seminarians, or spend the evening talking with friends from the Harlem neighborhood. Or I might return to the tenement to read or write; or, more often than not, do a little more work in rehabilitating the place, go out late to get the *Times,* and visit with people on the streets. I crossed a lot of boundaries in the course of a day. That in itself is not so important. What is *very* important is that in crossing boundaries of class and race and education and all the rest, a man remain himself. What is important is not where a man is, but who a man is, and that he be the same man wherever he is.

I recall one day in the tenement when a young curate from my parish stopped by to call. A boy from the neighborhood was there; we had just been talking about one of the gangs. The curate happened to be a graduate of Union Theological Seminary in New York. The previous day I had received an invitation to give a lecture at the seminary. The invitation pleased me, partly because I have a continuing disagreement with some of the faculty there, and I welcomed the opportunity to state my own views publicly at the seminary. In the conversation with the curate, in the presence of the boy, I remarked face-

tiously, "I have an invitation from the seminary to give a
lecture—now I will have a chance to speak in the heart of
the enemy camp!"

Subsequently, on the day of the lecture, just as it was
about to begin, the boy who had heard this remark entered the classroom, walked down the aisle, and seated
himself in the front row. After I had delivered the lecture
—about the relationship of Christ and law as described in
the Letter to the Colossians—there were several questions
from the seminarians, many of whom were manifestly
antagonistic to the views I had presented. Two or three
times during this discussion, after hostile questions had
been asked, the boy passed me notes to reassure me, by
charming if obscene comments about those who asked
the questions. I thought to myself that the boy had taken
seriously my crack about being in the "enemy camp" and
had come to the lecture to be a sort of bodyguard. That
was a great comfort.

Later, the boy and I returned together on the bus to
Harlem. On the way, he talked about the lecture and the
seminary, and he said: "That was nice—you talked to
them the same way you talk to me."

That was an even greater comfort.

The issue for any man, in any place, is to be the same
man he is in every other place. It was that issue which I
joined in a conclusive way while I was in the Army. It
was the resolution of that issue which made simple and,
so to speak, natural, the years in Harlem and which authorized the crossing of many boundaries.

The Piety of Poverty

For all the differences between Harlem and the rest of
the city of New York, for all the differences between Har-

lem and the image of American society, Harlem is nonetheless not unique. On the contrary, Harlem is plainly
representative of the congestion and destitution in which
most people in most of the world, through most of history
and even nowadays, live. Harlem in its own indigence
represents the outcast and the refugee and the homeless
and the hungry and the rejected and the forgotten everywhere else in the world. Harlem is the reminder and witness in American society of all the world's poor.

Those who are not poor need to remember the poor,
not just because there are so many poor people, not just
because, in fact, most people are poor, and not merely
because the poor are usually forgotten. Those who are
not poor need to remember the poor for *their* very own
sakes, not for the sake of the poor. They need to remember the poor because, curiously enough, the poor represent them, too.

It should be obvious that the poor represent exactly
those whose immediate victims they are: the slum landlord, the scab employer, the insolent municipal bureau-
crat, the shyster merchant, the loan shark, the bribable
building inspector, the corruptible cop, the paternalistic
politician, and the whole array of parasites whose own
power or profit or status or livelihood depends upon the
continuance of poverty. The travail of the poor is inter-
cessary for the rich—for *them,* in their behalf, in their
place, it substitutes for their own suffering. They would
suffer if the poor did not purchase for them some immunity from suffering.

Less obviously perhaps, but nonetheless, the poor—in
the very aggravation of their own lot—make up for and
minimize the suffering of those whose wealth is not apparently culpable, those who are not explicitly parasites
of poverty. Now I know that all men suffer in their apparent bondage to death, and I know that there are other
kinds of suffering than the deprivations and trials of pov-

erty, but here I only emphasize, not the exclusiveness, but the acuteness of the suffering of the poor. Nor do I imply by this that every affliction of the poor is innocent, because it is not so, either empirically or theologically. I only point out the service of the poor, in *their* suffering —to all those who suffer less, or differently—to all those who are not poor. All men, in short, live in a history in which every action and omission and abstention is consequentially related to all else that happens everywhere. That is the theology of Adam's Fall and with him, the fall of all men. In history, men live at each other's expense.

What sophisticates the suffering of the poor is not innocence, nor extremity, nor loneliness, nor the fact that it is unknown or ignored by others; but, rather, the lucidity, the straightforwardness with which it bespeaks the power and presence of death among men in this world. The awful and the ubiquitous claim of death is not different for the poor than for other men, or, for that matter, for nations or ideologies or other principalities or powers; but among the poor there are no grounds to rationalize the claim, no way to conceal the claim, no facile refutation of the claim, no place to escape or evade it.

Among the poor, men know that the estrangement between themselves and the rest of creation is so radical and fearsome that it seems explicable only in terms of the subjection of men and the rest of creation to death. Among the poor, the relationship between men and the rest of the creatures which have been made, which is the relationship of work, is no longer one of dominion but one of servitude, in which the man, the worker, becomes the object, becomes a mere (and frequently expendable) mechanism, with little or no reward save that which is already encumbered by debt. Among the poor, men literally work to death.

Some do not work at all; they do not have even that.

Among them, the lost relationship between men and the rest of creation is perhaps even more clearly a foretaste of and a tribute to the power of death. Nonwork is as much a burden as work.

What sophisticates the suffering of the poor is only the proximity of their life to death every day.

But the apparent conclusiveness of death yields in the common life of the poor a most remarkable social morality. Consider, for one example, the morality of gang society among East Harlem adolescents. Gang society nurtures a morality which induces members actually to risk their lives for each other and for their society and for causes which outsiders would think unworthy—like jurisdiction over a street that is filled with garbage or over a girl who probably is not a virgin. They risk their lives for apparently unworthy purposes. That is practically the opposite of the morality of the rest of American society, in which few would actually think of giving up their own lives for another, much less for that which seems unworthy. But these kids somehow apprehend a different way: They have the freedom to offer their lives for another, in spite of the undeservingness of the one for whom the offer is made. That is strangely reminiscent of the Gospel, in which One offers His life for all, even though none are worthy of His life.

Social morality is just another term for piety. The proximity of the poor to death matures a radical and wonderful piety, constituted in the actual life of the poor and consisting of the intense humility of the poor about their own existence as human beings. As the Ninth Psalm says, among the poor, men know that they are but men.

Any who work among the poor need constantly to realize the piety which is inherent in poverty; otherwise their work will be pretentious and manipulative, and the poor have enough to suffer without the further indignity of being the pawns of conventional charity. Too many people are murdered in the name of the charity which is done to them and for them.

Conventional charity, whether governmental or voluntary, like all aspirations of men to discern and do what is good, can cope only partially, impersonally, temporarily, superficially, piecemeal, with the issues which assail the poor. It is impotent against the fundamental reality represented in each of those issues, that is, the threat of death, not only eventually, but on every side in every single moment. The awful vulnerability of the poor is, in fact, the common vulnerability of every man to the presence and power of death in the world. And from the power of death, no man may deliver his brother, nor may a man deliver himself.

Yet it is exactly to the giving over of all men and all of creation and all of history to the power of death, to which the Christian faith is addressed. Christians confess that the whole burden of human existence in all of its variety is death, and insist that the stark, relentless activity of death in all the works of men—even the works which men imagine to be good—must be confronted, not ignored. Indeed, Christians see that death is the substance and outcome of the estrangement of men from God, and within that, of the separations among men and of the hostility between men and the rest of creation. •

• To become and to be a Christian is not at all an escape from the world as it is, nor is it a wistful longing for a "better" world, nor a commitment to generous charity, nor fondness for "moral and spiritual values" (whatever that may mean), nor self-serving positive thoughts, nor persuasion to splendid abstractions about God. It is, instead, the knowledge that there is no pain or privation, no humiliation or disaster, no scourge or distress or destitution or hunger, no striving or temptation, no wile or sickness or suffering or poverty which God has not known and borne for men in Jesus Christ. He has borne death itself on behalf of men, and in that event He has broken death itself on behalf of men, and in that event He has broken the power of death once and for all.

That is the event which Christians confess and celebrate and witness in their daily work and worship for the sake of all men.

To become and to be a Christian is, therefore, to have the extraordinary freedom to share the burdens of the daily, common, ambiguous, transient, perishing existence of men, even to the point of actually taking the place of another man, whether he be powerful or weak, in health or in sickness, clothed or naked, educated or illiterate, secure or persecuted, complacent or despondent, proud or forgotten, housed or homeless, fed or hungry, at liberty or in prison, young or old, white or Negro, rich or poor.

For a Christian to be poor and to work among the poor is not conventional charity, but a use of the freedom for which Christ has set men free.

Chapter Two
ACCEPTANCE

It was late and 100th Street was dark.

I was returning from 96th and Lexington—the nearest newsstand open that carried The New York Times.

It was November and fairly cold, so the streets were mostly empty, but when I turned into East 100th Street, I noticed two figures, down the block. They noticed me, too.

When I got near them, one of the figures spoke to me.

It was Archie. He and I had talked many times about many things. Archie was a pusher—he sold narcotics—and sometimes we had talked about his rights, legally, should he ever be arrested. He is part Negro, part Puerto Rican. He is married to a woman with whom he seldom stays. Archie is always busy hustling, in one way or another.

Anyway, he recognized me as I approached, and called my name and said to come over. I did.

"I want you to meet Bill," he said to his girl friend.

She was a young Negro woman, dressed a little shabbily, but in a way that wasn't too noticeable.

"He's my friend," Archie continued, talking to the girl. Archie looked me straight in the eye and then turned to the girl and ordered:

"Take care of him whenever he wants it."

I shook Archie's hand and went home.

I knew I had been accepted.

There was nothing romantic or idealistic or heroic, as far as I am concerned, about the decision to go to Harlem to live and work.

The idea of going there, as I have said, was not my own, but George Todd's, and I was as much influenced, I think, by the prospect of having Todd as a working colleague in cases and in neighborhood politics and in the life of the Church as anything else. Todd and I had been friends for a long time, and though we had attended different schools, we had remained in contact and in conversation during the years since we first met in the World's Student Christian Federation. Todd is a marvelously passionate person. He is not a religious man, caring as the religious do, only for his own salvation. He is a Christian, a man whose love for the Word of God embraces his affirmation of the lives of others. Todd enjoys the Gospel, and he knows that the place where the Gospel is to be lived is in the world. After finishing at Yale Divinity School, Todd had come to Harlem and engaged in his ministry in the neighborhood, and when he proposed that I do the same, I trusted his counsel and gave it great weight.

The prospect of practicing law in Harlem had, of course, to be considered in relation to other opportunities which presented themselves during my last year in law school. One possibility was to return home—to Northampton—where it would have been possible either to join an established firm or open my own practice, and where there were certain political opportunities which commended themselves. There was also the possibility of joining a large Boston firm with an excellent and interesting practice. But my experience in law school had been such as to interest me mainly in courses and cases which involved direct contact with clients—and, at that, with clients who are people, not institutions. The Boston practice would not have provided that. There was also an invitation to work for The Church Society for College Work of the Episcopal Church, in a ministry devoted to law students and faculty, focused upon the meaning of the Christian vocation for lawyers. However, it seemed to me that I would first have to practice law for a while before such an undertaking full time would make sense, though subsequently I have engaged in such work part time.

While I pondered these and other alternatives, Todd came to see me in Cambridge and made his suggestion that I come to Harlem to practice law there in collaboration with the parish. I visited the Harlem neighborhood, met some of those who would be my associates, talked with the clergy of the parish, and finally decided to settle there myself.

I knew that there was little money to be made in practicing in Harlem, but I had never had much money anyway and, as the rich gratuitously complain, had never had to suffer the burden of wealth. I was born during the depression and remember that my father, a knitter in the hosiery industry, was often out of work for long periods of time. After the depression waned, the hosiery industry was radically changed by the introduction of nylon, and, in the consolidation of the industry that ensued, many firms, including the one for which my father worked, moved South to take advantage of tax concessions and cheaper labor. Poverty for white working-class Americans is not nearly as profound economically, socially, or psychologically as it is for urban Negroes. As a child I was not really aware that we were poor. It was only when I was in high school and first talked with my parents about going to college that I realized that my family could not afford a college education for me and that if I wanted one I would somehow have to pay for it pretty much by myself. So I did. It was, I think, far easier for me to do it than it would be for a Negro boy. I had no difficulty getting jobs, after school and in the summers. In fact, during my senior year in high school I managed three jobs simultaneously—one picking asparagus before dawn, another as a stock clerk in a store in the afternoons, and then, at night, as a soda jerk in the ice-cream parlor where most of the kids hung out. Moreover, the school I attended was an excellent one academically and had teachers who took great interest in their students. Scholarship opportunities were available. Before I graduated from high school, I had a choice of three scholarships. The fact that my family was relatively poor did not affect, in any way that I can see, our social relationships in the community while I was growing up. A good many of my friends and playmates were from families of some wealth and social prominence, though I do not recollect that any of us even thought about such matters. In short, the poverty familiar to the families of white industrial workers in America in times of depression and high unemployment is not nearly so confining and dehumanizing as the poverty of the black ghettos. We were poor, but I was not deprived. We were poor, but I could go to college. We were poor, but I was readily accepted in the homes of the rich. We were poor, but I could "pass" in white bourgeois society. We were poor, but I had a chance. That is not the way it has been for most Negroes in America.

In any case, not being much accustomed to money, it was no particular sacrifice to move to Harlem. There was nothing to be given up economically in going there. I had savings of about $1,800—and that's all. And, not being bred to wealth or class, there was nothing in my inheritance as a person to repudiate psychologically in moving to Harlem.

To decide to live and work in Harlem was an essentially simple decision for me.

Remember the Outcast

The main reason for the decision was that I had come to feel—I suppose that I had been indoctrinated at law school—that the health and maturity of the American legal system depend upon whether or not those who are the outcasts in society—the poor, the socially discriminated against, the politically unpopular—are, as a practical matter, represented in their rights and complaints and causes before the law. Harlem seemed to be a place where a lawyer might find out something about that issue, and so I decided to go there.

To be concerned with the outcast is an echo, of course, of the Gospel itself. Characteristically, the Christian is to be found in his work and witness in the world among those for whom no one else cares—the poor, the sick, the imprisoned, the misfits, the homeless, the orphans and beggars. The presence of the Christian among the outcasts is the way in which the Christian represents, concretely, the ubiquity and universality of the intercession of Christ for all men. All men are encompassed in the ministry of the Christian to the least of men. I had to find out more about the meaning of that, too.

What I found out—what I found out theologically—from my stay in Harlem is, of course, that all men are outcasts in one sense or another. It is only more vivid that men are outcasts in a place like Harlem. No man, however, escapes this condition; no man avoids alienation from other men; no man evades the Fall.

Unhappily, what I found out is that, for the most part, the outcasts of this society—those who live somehow on its fringes—are not usually or effectively or even honestly represented before the law. Most are simply not represented at all. They can't afford the law, or they are so uninformed as to their rights that they do not pursue them, or they are so disenchanted by what they know or hear of the administration of the law that they have no confidence that their rights will be vindicated.

Those that are represented are too often the victims of charlatan attorneys who win cases by fixing them in one way or another, and who may milk their clients in order to pay the price for such a result. In many cases, of course, the client depends upon charity for his legal representation, and resorts to Legal Aid. I have a high regard for the work of the Legal Aid Society lawyers in New York, but the fact is that they are grossly overworked. Lawyers on their staff handle nearly seventy thousand cases each year, and, as far as I can observe, handle them as well as could be expected under such an enormous case load. God knows how many other tens of thousands of cases were forfeited because there were neither Legal Aid lawyers nor private lawyers willing or able to accept these cases.

Be all that as it may, the overriding truth is, as I have somewhat ruefully discovered, that most people who live in places like Harlem are not represented before the law. In many instances, moreover, the administration and practice of the law in this society works against the securing of their rights under the law, just because they are poor, or just because they are Negroes, or just because they are dependent upon conventional charity, or just because they do not know what their rights are in the first place.

Fairly soon in my Harlem practice I realized that those who are outcast, so far as society and the law are concerned, are not only the poor or those discriminated against in society because of race. More and more, I began to be asked to handle a variety of unpopular cases.

For instance, some years ago there was a call asking if I would undertake to represent a man who was seeking the restoration of his American citizenship, which he had renounced just prior to the Second World War to become a German citizen and a member of the Nazi Party in wartime Germany. The case was referred to me, I was told, because it was known that I sometimes defended narcotics addicts and might, therefore, be willing to take this other extremely unpopular case (which I did). A number of pacifists and peace demonstrators have also come for legal assistance. One case involved a group of people who were proposing to demonstrate in Times Square against nuclear testing, and who came to me to seek advice about how they might legally demonstrate and picket in New York City. I told them the law, indicating what activities they might engage in without liability to arrest. They listened to me and went away. A few days later, they held their demonstration protesting nuclear testing, during which some of them did exactly what I had advised them would be likely to result in their arrest. They were, in fact, arrested, and I subsequently defended some of them on trial. After many postponements, the cases were heard and the defendants received suspended sentences for the offenses of which, in my judgment, according to the law as it is now, they were clearly guilty. After the hearings, I received a call from one of the defendants complaining that he had received a suspended sentence instead of a jail term! He explained at some length that he had, after all, suffered a loss of prestige within the peace movement by getting off so easily for his deliberate civil disobedience.

There have been a good many other cases and different kinds of cases, too, beyond the limits of Harlem, which involve what might be called outcasts of society: for example, as counsel for The George Henry Foundation, which specializes in cases of sexual offenders in New York City, and in representing, with other counsel, some of the

Freedom Riders in Southern jurisdictions. As far as I can see, these two types of cases, along with those of the peace demonstrators, involve very similar issues. In each instance the arrest is typically for disorderly conduct endangering a breach of the peace. In each case the chief issue is whether the police are justified in arresting the accused because the accused's conduct is jeopardizing the peace. In each case the issue of the use or abuse of police discretion is involved. In other words, in my own view, from my own experience, the arrests of sexual offenders and peace demonstrators in New York parallel and present the same issues legally—and morally—as those involving civil rights demonstrators in Mississippi or Alabama, and both of the former types of cases are, in principle, as important, from the point of view of the fairness, maturity, and impartiality of the American legal system, as the more explicit and obvious civil rights cases.

In any event, the general picture is that neither the social minorities within the Harlem ghetto or in the South, nor the social minorities—such as sexual offenders and peace demonstrators—who are more or less at large in the outer city, are to any significant extent adequately represented before the law. As the unpopular and alienated are inadequately represented before the law, so are the legal rights of all citizens placed in jeopardy, because even the least are promised the equal protection of the law.

Existentialism in the Practice of Law

Given the widespread neglect by established society, including the legal profession, of the outcasts, and particularly the outcasts of the urban slums, how does one begin, as a person and as a lawyer, to reach and serve these people?

My own recollection is of having no particular rules or

strategy about how to be accepted, trusted, and thus used
as a lawyer in Harlem. If I had any rules or deliberate
tactics, they were very simple. I decided in advance that
I would speak to no one, take no initiative in making a
relationship with anyone, but just live there as long as I
had to until I was noticed and until someone sought me
out. It is true that I had both the advantage and disad-
vantage of coming to the neighborhood, initially, under
the patronage of the East Harlem Protestant Parish. That
meant that through the parish and its staff, I met a certain number of people fairly quickly and easily. But,
mainly, I was on my own. And I decided that I would
make no independent overture to anyone, for after all *I*
was the outsider, entering, probably intruding, upon the
lives of these people, and if they would welcome me and
accept me, that was up to them. There was nothing I
could or should do, apart from just being myself and being present among them day after day.

For quite a long time—for two or three months—I did
not speak to anyone, nor did anyone speak to me, though
I saw many people from the block and the neighborhood
and though they recognized and watched me.

Then, one night a boy called Monk came to see me. I
had seen him before around the block and knew that he
was the war counselor of one of the gangs. He said he
had heard that I was living in the neighborhood and that
I was a lawyer, and he said that a friend of his was in
trouble with the law and he wanted to ask me a few questions. I welcomed him. We had some beer and talked. It
quickly became apparent that his friend with the legal
problem did not exist. This was just a story, an excuse by
which the boy could come to see me and talk with me and,
I suppose, size me up. He stayed about three hours and
we talked about many things. We got along fine. The next
morning I walked over to Hell Gate post office, about
twelve blocks away, and as I went back to 100th Street,

I was stopped and greeted by ten or twelve of the boys who were on the street. They were friendly and knew my name and told me theirs. After our meeting the previous night, Monk evidently had vouched for me.

Thereafter I felt welcome on the street, spent more time there, and many of the people—not only the boys, but some of the older people—would wait around until I came along to discuss legal matters of all sorts, as well as gossip about the news and happenings of the neighborhood. The street became as much of an office as I ever had in Harlem.

The street is perhaps an unorthodox place to counsel clients, but whatever the inconveniences of such a practice, there were advantages as well. For one thing the overhead was very low. Moreover, I admit enjoying the freedom of wearing chinos and sneakers while practicing law. I remember one afternoon going to the northern part of East Harlem to visit an old woman who was having difficulties with the welfare authorities. The matter took several hours to settle, and by the time I was returning to East 100th Street, it had turned rather cold. I had gone out in the afternoon, when it was warmer, dressed only in a shirt, chinos, and sneakers, but now that the weather had changed, I was shivering from the cold. About two blocks from my tenement, a boy I knew, who had been loafing on the corner, called out that he wanted to ask me something. As we talked he saw that I was freezing to death and so he took off his jacket and gave it to me to wear. The boy is an addict and I happened to know that the clothes on his back were virtually the only ones he had—he had pawned everything else. Sometimes, when his clothes were being laundered, he would have to stay in the house because he had nothing else to wear, unless he could borrow something from someone. But he saw that I was cold and gave me his jacket. That is what is known as a sacrament.

Practicing law in Harlem has some similarities to small-town practice. The differences between the inner city and the outer city induce and enforce an intense localism and immobility. Many of my neighbors, especially women and younger children, seldom left the block. The localism, the attachment to one block, is sanctioned by apprehension about places that are unknown or unfamiliar, but it is also sanctioned by a sense of being unwelcome anywhere but on the block where one lives. I found, for example, that grocery prices were higher generally in the little stores in my immediate neighborhood, and so I used to go five blocks south—across the border and outside of East Harlem—to buy food at a supermarket. Several times I asked women on the block why they did not do the same and thereby save a little money, but the answer was usually that the place where I shopped was "a white man's store," though an additional factor is the relatively easy credit extended by the stores on the block.

The cases which arise in a law practice such as this are usually acutely personal: family squabbles, truancy, desertions, addiction, abandoned children, gang fights, evictions, securing repairs or heat or light from a slum landlord, intervening with the welfare investigators, legitimizing children, stopping repossession of furniture, complaining about police abuse of persons arrested. Legal counseling in such cases is as much a vehicle of pastoral care as it is of the practice of law.

To practice law in Harlem requires more than a professional identification with these kinds of cases. It involves more than knowledgeability about the neighborhood, and something different from just sympathy for the people of the ghetto. Humanitarian idealism is pretentious in Harlem, and turns out to be irrelevant. It is, rather, more important to experience the vulnerability of daily life. It is necessary to enter into and live within the ambiguity, and risk the attrition of human existence. In a way, it is even more simple than that: It is just essential to become and to be poor.

I do not say this in a moral sense, but exactly the contrary; I do say it in a theological sense and, therefore, in the most concrete and most practical sense (for unlike philosophic morality, theology deals with the care of God for all men in the common life of the world as it actually is now, while morality deals with some ideal life out of this world). As a practical matter, then, it is essential to share life just as it is in a place like Harlem. It is the only way there is to honor the Incarnation. In some other situations, I suppose that it might be possible for a lawyer simply to be a technician, but cases in Harlem almost invariably require face-to-face encounter with a client. For that communication, it is important to have known the client as a person before the case arose, to have seen or met or talked with him around the neighborhood, to have accepted him and to have been accepted by him, to have lived in the same place and similar circumstances as his own, and to expect a continued relationship after the particular case, as such, is closed.

This has been repeatedly confirmed, I have observed, in the lower criminal and family courts in New York: there is apt to be a very great similarity in the facts from case to case; and the enormity of the daily case load prevents the judge or the attorney or the probation officer from knowing much more about a party than his name and the most abbreviated version of the facts. I recall one case in family court where my client and I conferred with the probation officer for about twenty minutes prior to the hearing. Afterwards, the officer told me that in the six years she had been assigned to this court, ours was the longest interview she could recall. Where such circumstances prevail, the hearing and disposition of a case are a mere ritual; they are no longer the administration of the law.

But if a lawyer must himself be immersed in the life of the place where he practices, then the law itself must be genuinely implicated in and wrought from the realities of human existence. That would help to free the law from pretentious moralism and from superstition and obsolescence as well. The operation of the rent control law against the interests of the very people it was intended to protect, as already mentioned, is just one example of the obsolescence which results when the law grows out of touch with practical life.

Another instance is narcotics legislation. Many of my clients are young narcotics addicts apprehended in possession of drugs for their own use. (Use of drugs is not in itself a crime.) The law condemns mere possession of addicting drugs as a criminal offense, failing to make any distinction between the commercial pusher in possession for traffic and the addict in possession for personal use. The legal inference attached to mere possession is that drugs are possessed for the purpose of illegal transfer rather than use. Apparently, popular sentiment disregards this distinction and also superstitiously envisions the addict as a fiend prone to violent antisocial behavior. Yet addicts are often fairly tranquil, and there is impressive medical authority that addiction is an illness, certainly as clearly as alcoholism is, requiring medical supervision and psychiatric therapy. Penal confinement of the addict who is not a pusher is even less defensible, because of the shortage of professional staff and facilities for hospitalization and rehabilitation of addicts in prison. Nor are there usually provisions to care for addicts immediately upon their arrest; instead, they commonly have to endure going "cold turkey"—that is, the convulsive agony of abrupt and absolute withdrawal from drugs.

Not only is the law obsolete in this instance and indifferent to crucial facts about the matter with which it purports to deal, but I would argue that it works vindictively.

One client of mine is now in prison for the sixth time in about as many years, for an offense related to his addiction. He was caught stealing a typewriter from a Roman Catholic monastery, and received a very stiff sentence, mainly, I think, because the theft was from a church. (I told him after he was sentenced that next time, if he had to break into a church, please pick a Protestant church, and then, maybe, I could fix it!) For him, there has been no remotely competent treatment for his addiction while in prison, and the stigma of his convictions for narcotics offenses cuts off other possible remedies. When he is released, it will be practically impossible for him to secure employment; neither public nor private counseling agencies specialize in, or have much experience in, addiction cases, save for a couple of experimental agencies. Practicing psychiatrists cost a great deal of money and the amateur analysis and therapy of social workers and ministers risk more harm than help. He has no friends outside the city to whom he can turn and no means to go to them if he had; his father has disavowed him as a son. His only alternative is to return to the streets—and so the cycle continues, deepening his frustration, breaking his morale, aggravating his self-preoccupation, ruining his health, destroying his personality, accelerating the prospect that he will return again to drugs, increasing the probabilities of another arrest and imprisonment.

For him, and for many more, the law and the enforcement of the law represent a special jeopardy, just because he is poor. An addict with income enough to pay for private care and for medical supervision of his use of drugs —and there are plenty of them—runs relatively little risk of arrest. It is the addict who is poor, who lives on the street, who, once arrested, is under close police scrutiny, who deals with a pawnbroker (for whom it may be convenient or profitable to tip off the police), who must resort to theft to buy a "fix," who has to be wary of other addicts

who may exchange his arrest for theirs, who has no privacy, no place to hide—that is the addict who is arrested
again and again. Yet he is the least important arrest that
could be made, the most expendable link in the narcotics
traffic; he pays the lowest price for stuff which is adulter-
ated anyway; he probably has contact with one minor
operator in the astonishingly intricate narcotics syndicate.
But he is the easiest to arrest, under the present law, and
so, it seems, some police are willing to let the pushers—not
to mention higher-ups in the narcotics traffic—go free and
pursue only the addicts.

Generally speaking, while the people of the neighborhood are not well informed about their legal rights or
about legal procedures (and therefore are often unwit-
tingly deprived of their rights, or default in pursuing remedies to which they are legally entitled), this is not so much
the case with the addicts. They are arrested so often that
they become fairly sophisticated as to the law as it directly
affects them and also as to how a given case is likely to be
decided. My first case in court, as a novice in law practice,
was one in which an addict was the defendant and my
client. He and three other boys were in a certain tenement
apartment when it was raided by the police, who had apparently been tipped off by another addict that drugs
could be found in the apartment. The latter boy had been
picked up on the street by the police and, in order to save
himself from arrest, had evidently informed on the boys
in the apartment. The police broke into the place and
found the four boys in the kitchen with a paper bag con-
taining heroin on the table. All were arrested on the
charge of illegal possession of narcotics. Whether such a
charge is a felony or a misdemeanor depends, in part,
upon the amount of narcotics in possession. In this case,
chemical analysis proved that the amount was sufficient
to warrant a felony charge if the "stuff" belonged to just
one of the boys arrested. If, however, the four jointly and

equally owned the drugs, then the charge against each would be only a misdemeanor. I interviewed all of the boys and am satisfied that they had all participated in the procurement of the drugs and were partners in its possession and intended use. But they had decided among themselves that it would be best if, as they put it, just one of them "took the weight." As they saw it, it was better for one to plead that the stuff was entirely his own and therefore be charged with a felony and risk a long prison sentence than for each of them to admit part ownership and each be charged with a misdemeanor, with the prospect of much shorter sentences for each.

This is the version they told the police after their arrest and before I entered the case; and this is the story they stuck to, so far as the police were concerned. Consequently, by the time the case came to me, three of the boys had been released; the fourth remained in custody on the felony charge. He had been elected to take the weight so that his friends could go free. It was a crude, but genuine, act of intercession.

There was no real defense for the addict who remained under arrest; he had been caught in possession of illegal drugs. There was the issue of whether the raid on the apartment constituted an illegal search and seizure, but after considering that awhile and discussing the issue with several more experienced lawyers, I concluded that there was little or no prospect of prevailing on that issue in the court of original jurisdiction, though there might be a chance of success in an appellate court. There were, however, no funds for an appeal, and it was not, after all, a strong search and seizure case to begin with, given the tip upon which the police had acted. The defendant had a record of three previous convictions—all of them related to his addiction—and it appeared that it was the fact that his record was the worst that caused his selection to take the weight.

On the day the case came up for pleadings, I left my tenement early and walked down 100th Street. The other three boys were hanging around on the steps of one of the tenements. I stopped to talk with them. They knew where I was going and said they had been waiting for me, to wish me luck and to give me a message for their friend. They asked me what I planned to do in court. I had decided, partly on the advice of another attorney, to go to court before it convened and discuss the case with the prosecutor and try to persuade him to reduce the charge, in exchange for a guilty plea. There were not any serious legal grounds for the district attorney to agree to this, but there were practical arguments in favor of it. For one thing, the defendant had been in prison three other times, and since this had not deterred his addiction, there was no reason to think that a long felony sentence would be of any help to him or advantage to society. For another thing, there is a shortage of prison space in New York, and that constitutes a pressure on the courts to hand down short sentences, at least in minor cases, which is what this was, even though it was a felony charge. In other words, what does society gain by filling the jails with addicts rather than real criminals? Moreover, it seemed to me that the chief interest in the enforcement of the law in such cases as this was the making of the arrest, not the actual disposition of the case. Then, too, there was the consideration that by pleading guilty to a lesser offense, the court would be saved the time and expense of holding the prisoner for trial, of the trial itself, and of the trouble of any further proceedings in the matter.

The defendant's friends seemed sure that the lesser charge would prevail with the district attorney and the court, though in my naïveté, I remained doubtful whether it would or whether it should. One of the boys that morning even ventured to predict that the defendant would get no more than a six months' sentence. That seemed to me too short to hope for, but, having made a decision in what I considered to be radically ambiguous circumstances, I determined to stick to it and went off to court to talk with the district attorney.

When I arrived at the court room, several other lawyers were standing in line, waiting to speak to the D.A. I overheard their discussions of other cases on the day's calendar. They were terse, to say the least, and seemed to me to be quite disinterested and even indifferent to the merits of the cases being negotiated. Finally my turn came. I identified myself to the district attorney, whom I had never met before, this being my first court case.

I told him whom I represented, and then he said, "Well, counselor, what do you want?" "I want a misdemeanor," I replied. And then to my astonishment he said, "O.K. When the case is called, we'll talk to the judge."

We did. The judge agreed to the guilty plea to a misdemeanor, and the defendant was sentenced to seven months in prison.

It was all over in no more than two minutes. After the hearing, I went back to the "pen"—where the prisoners are kept, pending their appearance in court and awaiting their return to jail—and talked with the defendant. He was very pleased with the way the case had gone. He assured me that this was the best solution, certainly better than for all four of them to be imprisoned. Besides, he said, he knew how to get along in jail, and some of the other guys did not, so it was better that he should go in their place. I gave him the message from his friends, and he asked me to give them a reply. And then he was taken away and I left.

I did not return immediately to East Harlem, but walked around awhile in lower Manhattan, thinking about what had happened that morning. What I had observed about the practical administration of the law bore almost no relationship that I could identify to what I had learned

in law school. And it had all gone so easily. I did not have
to persuade anybody, either the D.A. or the court, that
the charge should be reduced. I just had to go in and ask
for it. It all seemed wrong—some great sham was being
made of the law and of the legal system. Yet it all seemed
right. The arrest in the first place was a waste of time, so
far as the narcotics issue was concerned, and prison, even
for these few months, was not going to change my client's
way of life, so why shouldn't he get off as easily as possible?
Maybe the issue is that the law as it deals with the possession of narcotics is a stupid law and proves itself in this
way. Even so, what of other laws? Are they enforced
and administered the way this one was? Is the law, in
practice, this subjective and manipulative? On the other
hand, maybe this amounts to some rough and ready sort
of justice. Maybe this and maybe that—a million maybe's.
Maybe this is just the kind of world that is: upside down,
broken, foolish, wasteful, absurd, and filled with irony.
Maybe so.

In all events, I now felt baptized as a lawyer.

I was—as a person—pleased that the sentence was short.
When I returned to East 100th Street that day, I found the
defendant's buddies again waiting on the street to find out
what had happened.

"Seven months," I told them. The one who had made
the prediction—six months—smiled at me and shook my
hand. "You're all right," he said.

Later on, after the defendant had been in prison for a
couple of months, I went to see him. I recall that the guard
who admitted me asked why I had bothered to come.
"Usually the lawyers don't come here," he announced.
"The case is over, you can't do anything for him here." "I
can visit him," I told the guard.

The inmate, I think, never looked better in his life—he
was clean, fed, and fairly content. He said that it was not
such a bad place to be and that he liked the regime of the

prison: he always knew when something was to be done; there was a structure to prison society to which he had known no parallel in his family or in Harlem, and he liked that about jail.

In many, many other cases, the same thing has happened: many inmates prefer prison society to the society of the slums. I have at this moment a client—an adolescent —in the City Penitentiary who is eligible for parole and who wrote me recently to ask that I make no effort to secure parole for him because he preferred to stay in prison as long as he could, rather than return to his home. To him, prison is less difficult and threatening, more secure and safe, than his own home and family, back in the slums. According to the doctors, this boy is deeply disturbed emotionally, and his preference for prison appears to be very much influenced by the estrangement between his parents and himself, particularly by the violent hostility between his father and himself. Let it be said, too, that the prison on Riker's Island where he is confined is equipped with an excellent physical plant, has a fine school, shops, library, infirmary, and athletic facilities and, for a prison, fairly spacious living quarters for the inmates. Being an island, it has no wall enclosing it. The administration of the prison, as far as I have had contact with it, is humane and genuinely oriented toward rehabilitation of the prisoners and their return to society. The trouble is that many have nothing to return to, or have at least much less to return to than what is provided or available in the penitentiary. In the ghetto there are no excellent physical surroundings, no fine schools, shops, libraries, hospitals, athletic facilities, or spacious living quarters. And those who become inmates at the penitentiary discover that they live in a city and society that empirically offers more in some ways to those who commit offenses against society and are imprisoned than to those who are innocent of offense against society and are legally free but confined to

the ghetto. No wonder such prisoners prefer jail to freedom. No wonder they speculate about what a strange
morality governs such a society.

Other cases, apart from those involving addicts, might
be cited as examples of the need for the law and the lawyer to be immersed in life as it is and to be free enough
from moralism, superstition, and obsolescence to cope
with it. Nowadays in New York's family court, social
workers, as a practical matter, replace not only legal counsel but judge and enforcement officer as well. And politics
supplants law in providing counsel for indigent defendants
in certain cases. In instances like these, the integrity of
the law and the work of the lawyer are usurped, because
both have become too isolated from actual life. Meanwhile, jurisprudence, instead of recalling the law—in legislation, administration, enforcement, adjudication, and
practice—to an appreciation of history and a deeper real-
ism about human existence, has dignified that isolation in
grandiose abstractions.

The fact that the law is usurped by other disciplines
and professions argues—contrary to a dictum I have heard
recited at the Harvard Law School—that the law cannot
be indifferent either to other disciplines in the university
or other professions in society. The argument is all the
more cogent because of the pluralism of American society,
for the accommodation of pluralism to freedom consists
not in the abolition or avoidance of controversy, but,
rather, in the maturity and quality of controversy under
the rule of law. (That is why genial, general tolerance
which ignores differences and disagreements and conflicts
among classes or races or factions in society is both un-
patriotic and sub-Christian.)

In short, the issue for the law is whether it exists within
the interstices of life, aware of the self-interest of adverse
contentions, free to be the advocate of each and all. For
that, the law and the lawyer must be radically exposed to

the existential situations of each party and person. To achieve this, even the outcast—perhaps especially the poor —must have counsel.

The Law as an Enemy of the Outcast

The poor need counsel, but more often than not, they are without counsel. This accounts in part for the suspicion and contempt in which the law is held by many who live in the ghettos. But it is not the only reason by any means.

The most frequent contact with the law which the inhabitants of Harlem and similar neighborhoods in the cities have is with the police. For many, the police are the only concrete image of the law they have ever known. The image that they see when they observe the police in action is of the law as an enemy—as a power which threatens, intimidates, oppresses, suppresses, and opposes their property and their lives.

The past summers have been ones of repeated incidents of violence against the police in Harlem and other "problem" areas of the city. The police have been stoned, struck, and otherwise assaulted. The police and the people of the slums are enemies. Yet are these incidents insolent, primitive acts of civil disobedience, or are they signs of radical hostility, accumulated grievance, and desperate protest against the treatment which Harlem Negroes—and Negroes in similar Northern ghettos in Chicago, Detroit, Boston, Philadelphia, and elsewhere—have come to assume that they will receive from the police and from the administration of the law? Who, after all, made the first assault—the police or the people? What about the sordid, persistent reports of shakedowns, bribes, and rigged arrests, not to mention police brutality and even sadism?

What about, for example, that Negro taken not long

ago to a Harlem police precinct and, it is said, interrogated so vigorously and viciously by the police that he later required treatment for brain concussion?

Why should any Harlem Negro obey the law or honor the rule of law who has seen the notorious, brazen, and unpunished countenance of, if not complicity of, the police in crap games, the numbers racket, procurement for prostitution, and the narcotics traffic?

Take the case of Hector, for example. Hector, a Negro, twenty-three years old, is of high intelligence, a pleasant appearance, and has a better education than many of his contemporaries from Harlem. He wants to be an actor. He had a long succession of menial jobs after he got out of school and from them saved a little money and migrated from Harlem to Greenwich Village. There he soon learned that opportunities to learn to act and to earn money were available to him if he made himself available to homosexuals. He is now in one of the acting schools, has his own Village apartment, has a part-time job in a store where he makes enough to manage, and has had a few small parts in Off Broadway productions. He has a chance to become an actor and to professionally succeed at it, though he may never be a star. One night he was arrested on a charge of disorderly conduct. His story is that about midnight he went out to get a newspaper a few blocks from where he had been visiting that evening, that he had paused on a certain corner, waiting for the traffic signal to change, when he was suddenly collared by a plain-clothes policeman and placed under arrest. The specific nature of his alleged disorderly conduct was that he was loitering in a public place for the purpose of soliciting a person of the same sex for an immoral purpose. I do not know if the arrest was justified or not. Hector admits to me that he is a homosexual, or at least that he has become a homosexual, in order to further his ambitions to act. At the same time, he insists that he said or did nothing that night to justify his arrest. Be that as it may, at the same corner, on the same night, at the same time, three other persons—all of them white men—were also arrested. All were taken together in the same police cruiser to the precinct station. At the station, Hector was separated from the others and interrogated separately from them, by a battery of three detectives. When he was being taken away, one policeman—a white man—said to Hector: "Get in there you black mother f----r." During Hector's interrogation by the three officers—all white —Hector asked, as is his right, to make a phone call. He says he was refused, but told that if he wished to send a message to someone, the police would take it and relay it. He gave the police the message to call his sister, who, as it happened, was then working as a secretary to a public official, and to tell her to call the official for whom she worked and inform him of the arrest. Hector's sister reports that the police did call her and tell her of Hector's arrest, but did not convey the message about calling her boss. After the call, according to Hector, the three officers returned to their interrogation of him, but the questions were no longer about the incidents involving the arrest. Now the questions took the vein: "Why do you want to reach him [the public official], Hector, why don't you call Malcolm X? He's your leader. Why don't you call him?" Hector says that he was taunted in this manner for nearly an hour, and that the interrogation was interrupted only when his sister arrived at the station and arranged for his release on bond.

I repeat that to this day I do not know for a certainty whether the arrest originally was justifiable or not, but I am satisfied that, once arrested, Hector was treated far differently by the police, verbally and physically, than the white defendants arrested under the same circumstances at the same time. How, then, can this man have any respect for the law when, in his direct contact with it, he found that he was not the equal of the white men with whom he was arrested?

It doesn't even have to go that far. Hardly a kid in Harlem, from the most tender years, has not observed a cop collecting a pay-off, overlooking an illegal crap game, talking with a known numbers man, arresting an addict instead of a pusher standing just across the street, going to a tavern for a free drink while on duty, or, sometimes, beating up somebody on the street.

One of the primary reasons for the low esteem in which Harlem's people hold the law is police brutality. I was skeptical when I first heard the stories of such brutality. Now, seven years later, there have been too many documented episodes of excessive and unnecessary violence initiated by the police against the citizens of Harlem for me to be skeptical any longer. I am sure—no, I hope —that some of the instances of police abuse are not true. I hope it is not as widespread as the rumors and reports indicate, but, on the other hand, I have had enough cases myself in which this was an issue to know that such charges against the police are not frivolous inventions.

A most distressing incident I know of involved a fight that took place one summer night between a young Negro and a young Puerto Rican. I have never really found out the cause of the fight, but I believe it was over a girl, an issue, after all, which has often been fought over and one which frequently is worth fighting over. The fight took place in the early evening on a street in the full view of a number of other people. There were plenty of witnesses. During the fight, two policemen, both white, came along and, as was their duty, broke up the fight. So far, so good. The boys were separated, searched, and interrogated. One boy, the Negro, who later became a client, refused to answer any questions except to tell the police his name and address. This is, of course, his right. In effect, he invoked the Fifth Amendment, although the evidence is that he did it with somewhat obscene language. The response of one of the policemen was to strike him so dreadfully that he fell to the sidewalk, whereupon, according to both the boy and several of the witnesses, the officer kicked him repeatedly in the face and groin. In due course, both boys were taken to the precinct house. Although a charge of felonious assault was a legally proper charge against both boys, only the Negro was so charged—and not only against the boy he had been fighting, but also against the very policeman who had beaten him.

Since the latter charge, given the facts as reported by the defendant, seemed without sufficient grounds, a great effort was made to locate and interview eyewitnesses who could either confirm or refute the boy's testimony. Of the many who were contacted and questioned, six (as I recall) essentially repeated the boy's own version of what had happened—that he had been assaulted by the policeman, rather than the other way around. Each of them admitted this in private conversation; none was willing to be a witness for the defense. They all had many excuses for their reluctance. They wanted to stay out of trouble —any trouble, all trouble, especially trouble involving the cops. It was none of their business, they kept saying. Clearly, they were afraid. These were the policemen from the beat; they would be around tonight and tomorrow and after that, and they might find something to arrest *you* for if *you* were going to be a witness against them in *this* case. Some had things to hide—illegal activities of their own— which argued against having anything to do with anybody else's problems with the law. Some—the most sympathetic —just had no confidence that, even if they did testify for the defense, their testimony (since they, too, were Negroes) would be given any credence by the court. They felt that since there was no chance for a fair and impartial

hearing and verdict, why take the time from work or home
to testify for this boy? His case was already decided—he
was a Negro. That settled it.

There were, in consequence, no witnesses for the defense respecting the policeman's alleged assault upon the
defendant. Even the defendant refused, despite urgent entreaties, to testify in his own defense. He viewed his case
as hopeless. Who would believe a Negro against a white
policeman? Entreaties are irrelevant to those whose experience is such that they no longer have any expectation that the law will protect them or regard them impar-
tially or honor their humanity.

Distrust and contempt for the law are further com-
pounded by incidents such as that involving Hector or the
one, just described, of the young Negro charged with as-
saulting an officer. Since he lives in an atmosphere of fear
and rumor, the repetition of these cases inevitably induces an exaggerated response and deepens the Negro's
sense that the law is an enemy.

If one needed further confirmation of this contention,
one would have only to consider one of the earliest riots in
New York's racial crisis. One night a fight in the street
broke out between the Negroes and the Puerto Ricans
living on one of the more crowded blocks. The fight had
begun as an argument between a Puerto Rican man and a
Negro woman, but it attracted the attention of their neighbors on the block, who then joined in the fighting, until
some two to three hundred people were involved. One
suspects that the real issue between the Negroes and the
Puerto Ricans in the riot was not the specific dispute
which touched off the incident, but the pent-up frustra-
tions of both peoples. Just too many people live there in
too little space and, especially, on sweltering summer
nights when it is too hot to sleep, it is not surprising that
there is impatience, short temper, argument, and fighting.

On this night, enough people participated to make it a riot, and before long the police arrived on the scene. When they arrived, the fighting between the Negroes and Puerto Ricans stopped and both turned upon the police, attacking them with beer cans and empty bottles. The Negroes and Puerto Ricans suffer much hostility between them, but the police represented the common enemy of both, and so they united against the police.

Police action of this sort, of course, feeds the cause of the radical racists in Harlem—the Black Muslims and the Nationalists—and makes the task of those Negro leaders who urge nonviolent action to secure jobs, decent housing, and civil rights more and more untenable in the minds of masses of people. No electric cattle prods have yet been used in Harlem, as they have in some cities in the Deep South, but plenty of Negroes have endured the blows of night sticks, and seen helmeted policemen breaking up demonstrations and carting scores off to jail. The image of the police (and of the law) is lamentably pretty much the same in New York as in Alabama, so far as Negroes and others who are poor or discriminated against are concerned: The police are an enemy, a sort of occupation force, representing the white power structure, engaged not in protecting but in oppressing the people. Nor do the people regard this as something new—something which began since the civil rights demonstrations were initiated —but, rather, they regard it as something that has been a reality for a very long time; indeed, ever since the people of the ghetto came into contact with the police and the administration of the law, in individual cases of false arrest and false charges, in countless instances of excessive force used by the police, and even in the courts, in the obstacles created there to obtaining a fair trial or the vindication of personal rights.

Even though such attitudes toward the police and the

law are based upon exaggeration in many instances, the significant fact is that they are believed. There is no doubt, however, that an overwhelmingly sufficient basis exists for the people of the ghetto to regard the law as their enemy.

Chapter Three
INVOLVEMENT

The meeting had been called to consider whether something might be done to expose and oppose police brutality in Harlem. There had been a noticeable increase in the number of incidents reported that summer, and the people of the community were provoked, angry, and restive.

About thirty people had been asked to the meeting. Some were clergymen, others journalists, a few were businessmen, two were in politics, some represented civil rights organizations, and some were attorneys. All, as it happened, were Negroes, except for myself.

I was late arriving at the meeting, which was held in central Harlem, having been in court all morning on a case, by coincidence, involving police abuse.

Most of those present were friends—by now we had worked together in a variety of matters and we knew and trusted each other. There were two persons present whom I had not yet met.

The chairman of the meeting interrupted the discussion when I came in and introduced me to the two to whom I was a stranger.

"This is Bill Stringfellow," she said, "he's a lawyer over in East Harlem. I've known him for five years.

"It's safe for us to talk in front of him."

In coming to Harlem, I was as much concerned about the politics in such a community and about the ministry of the Church in such a neighborhood, as in living and working as a lawyer there.

It was not very long before I was contacted by an emissary from the district political club, which at that time was affiliated with Tammany Hall. It was dominated by an Italian leadership, and had very few Negroes or Puerto Ricans as members. The man who made the contact told me that the club was aware I had moved into the neighborhood and had some sort of connection with the East Harlem Protestant Parish. (The parish had a reputation for active involvement in politics. One of its clergy had once run against the Tammany district leader, so the parish was not regarded very favorably by the political leadership of the club.) But, the man explained, they knew that I was a lawyer—not one of those ministers—and that, therefore, I might be more practical than the clergy and might wish to join the Tammany club instead of "making trouble" in the neighborhood, as some of the clergy had, he felt, been doing. He contended that everyone wanted to improve the neighborhood, but that the only way this could be done was by supporting the incumbent leader. After all, this was *his* district and if anything was to be done to change its conditions, the leader was the only one who could do it. "Nobody at City Hall will listen to anyone else from up here," he assured me. "Nobody else can get anything done."

He underscored his invitation to join the club as the "realistic" way to "get something done" for the neighborhood, with promise of some patronage. He claimed that

if I joined the club, and if I sought to keep the clergy from
interfering with things "they didn't know anything about,"
I would be put on the club's list of lawyers and thereby be
in line for appointment as counsel by the courts in certain
cases. For example, the state provides counsel fees in
capital cases for indigent defendants, and it is a common
practice for four or five lawyers to be appointed as defense counsel and then divide the fee among themselves.
Whether the defendant receives a competent defense in
instances where these appointments are a distribution of
patronage is, perhaps, open to question.

I told him that I appreciated the invitation, but was
obliged to decline it. And I went on to explain that politically speaking I was not in league with the clergy nor
responsible for any of their views or past actions, though
I would agree with some of them and not with others. Besides, I suggested somewhat sarcastically that if he wanted
to buy me with the offer of patronage, he would have to
begin by making a considerably better offer than the one
he had made.

He seemed to get the message. He knew, much better
than I, that if I had joined the club under the proposed conditions, I would have had no voice in the policy-making
of the club. There was only one man—the district leader
—who had such a voice. Membership in the club meant,
at most, access to the club premises to play cards and
drink whiskey and run errands for the boss and, maybe,
after doing this long enough to be trusted, there might be
a court appointment on a case worth a few hundred dollars. He seemed to understand that if I had any interest
in patronage, it would involve much more than he was
authorized to discuss.

After this encounter, the Tammany emissary and I became friends—of a sort; at least there was a candidness
in our relationship that I valued, and he knew that if I told
him something, it was the truth. In turn, I always found

him as good as his word. The fact that we disagreed radically about the political remedies appropriate to the district did not mean that we had to be enemies or to deceive each other on the occasions when we had to deal with each other.

The Politics of Poverty

As time went on, I learned a good deal more about the internal political life of the ghetto. Two or three times I served as a special deputy attorney general for the election frauds bureau of the State of New York, mainly in order to become more acquainted with politics.

Politics, my Tammany friend notwithstanding, has not provided even transient relief from poverty, much less a fundamental solution for poverty in Harlem.

At one time in East Harlem there was Vito Marcantonio, whose Congressional incumbency—whoever else backed him—rested in East Harlem upon personal service, not upon public policy. He found jobs, stayed evictions, arranged hospital care, secured legal aid. He is said to have had no less than sixteen storefront offices in the district open at night where people could come with their problems. When his services were surpassed by public welfare, private philanthropy, and social work, he fell. But though he is still remembered in East Harlem with esteem for all that he apparently did for people, Marcantonio, from what I can gather, was only a political personality, not a political boss, and there is little evidence that he threatened or cared to challenge the ruling political powers in East Harlem. He may, in one sense, have even served them well. By his flamboyance, he may have helped to distract people and encourage their political apathy, thereby leaving the spoils of city politics to the real bosses.

Significant political power in the city does not necessarily reside with those who occupy public office, especially in the Congress. It may well serve the vested interests of the political organization men to permit the election of a person to Congress, provided he tacitly agrees not to interfere with the political establishment. Such candidacies tend to sap the strength of reform factions and to divert the attention of voters and residents from the real centers of decision and power. Those centers of power rest neither upon personal service nor public policy, but essentially upon patronage. Patronage includes not only the bestowal of nominations for public office, state legislators, city councilmen, judgeships, and the like, but also the dispensing of municipal jobs of all sorts and at all echelons—including Sanitation Department employees and chauffeurs of city automobiles. Patronage also reaches into businesses outside the government which require licensing or the award of contracts by the city. Thus, in one case, a young Puerto Rican came to see me for help in securing a hack license. He was a veteran with an honorable discharge, a tested and capable driver, in good health, fully qualified for such a license. He had applied in the prescribed way, but he received no license and he was given to understand that no license would be issued to a Puerto Rican unless it was politically approved by a certain politician whose responsibility it was to dispense patronage—insofar as any was made available—to Puerto Ricans. Contact with the politician in question made it clear that a license could be obtained only if the applicant agreed to commit himself politically, as he was instructed, and to work in elections as he was told to do.

Similarly, there were anguished complaints in the primary campaign in which Adam Clayton Powell ran without Tammany endorsement, after a falling out with Carmine DeSapio (then leader of the Hall), and won, that he failed to use his victory to extract any significant patronage gains from DeSapio for Negroes. What Powell did get was the promise of support from the New York Democratic Congressional delegation for his fight to hold the Chairmanship of the House Labor Committee, which, by the traditions of seniority, he was entitled to receive but for which he was apparently opposed by some white Congressmen because he is a Negro. The patronage which Powell failed to bargain for and which some of his leading supporters in Harlem had sought was the award of insurance contracts on public housing projects. All such projects are required to carry insurance, and patronage evidently enters into the award of the contracts to insurance brokers. Negro insurance men wanted a share of this booty, but it appears that Powell had failed to seek or secure it for them. It appears that such complaints have not been lost to the congressman in view of his vigor in pursuing control of poverty programs for patronage.

In other words, the real foundation of political power is associated with the protection and preservation of vested economic interests in jobs of all sorts, in licensing and contracting, and, it is often rumored, in gambling, narcotics, and prostitution. In any event, where political power represents economic investment, whether lawful or criminal, the poor are apt to be excluded from politics, and ordinary citizens made unwelcome in active political life.

In Harlem, multitudes of citizens, both Negro and Puerto Rican, remain to this day practically disenfranchised. After all, the fewer people who are registered to vote, the fewer voters there are to control, and the fewer that have to be persuaded or purchased, or, after an election, listened to in their complaints and needs. In many election districts, far more people who could qualify to vote remain unregistered and unenrolled than those who are registered, and little or no effort is made by any party or faction to reach and register and enroll them, much less admit them to the councils of the local political clubs. The rise of the Negro revolt has, of course, begun to alter this to some extent, and more Negroes are turning out to register, but this is more attributable to the efforts of the civil rights organizations and to some of Harlem's churches than to the political parties. The impetus which the civil rights movement has given to voter registration is a probable explanation for the recent gerrymandering of certain Harlem districts in order to salvage, for as long as possible for as many white politicians and their accomplices, the old order in Harlem politics.

There are, of course, other factors which enforce the disenfranchisement of the people of the ghetto. One is the literacy test, which disqualifies many from voting and deters many others from trying to register. Another is the sheer effort and time required to register. When I registered, it took four hours to get to the place, go through the process and get back home—half of a working day. A lot of people can't afford to take the time off to do that. Others are skeptical that voting will change their life for the better in any appreciable way: They have heard the promises of politics too long and seen too few promises fulfilled to have confidence that politics will provide any real remedy. And if many are apathetic and cynical about the politics of the city, they are profoundly and furiously disillusioned with the two national parties and their unredeemed platform pledges on civil rights, housing, school integration, and equal treatment in public accommodations. All of this has meant that the poor are, in the main, unrepresented in the legislatures of the city, state, and nation. What their real needs and concerns may be are unknown and unheard of in the legislatures.

No significant legislative relief for narcotics addicts or for coping with the treatment of addicted persons has yet been effectively provided, either through the federal government or the governments of the State or City of New York. A few agencies and a few churches in New York City are concerned about the problem and have undertaken work among addicts, trying to provide them with legal assistance, psychiatric counseling, medical care, and job placement, as well as continuing to work for reform of the law. The Narcotics Committee of the East Harlem Protestant Parish, under the tenacious initiative of a minister, Norman Eddy, has doubtless been the city's pioneer in this work. But once again, as in the case of Father Gusweller already mentioned, a simply fantastic effort, sustained over a long period of time, has been necessary by Eddy and his associates in order to gain even a hearing from the civil authorities and the merest beginnings of legislative reform of the laws relating to narcotics.

It does not diminish the importance of such effort to point out that actual changes have been modest and begrudgingly granted. A procedure is now available for the medical, rather than penal, commitment of addicts. The problem remains of supplying adequate medical facilities for such committals. Under great pressure—including picketing and demonstrations at City Hall and the exposé of some of the issues by one of New York's newspapers—a few beds have been allotted in municipal hospital facilities for addicts. Meanwhile, approximately half the addicts in the nation live in New York City and about half of these live in Harlem. Estimates of their number run upwards of twenty thousand.

There is statutory authority for the State Commissioner of Public Health to designate hospital space for the treatment of addicts, but this has not been generally used, it seems, because of the public image it creates for a hospital to be identified as a place which treats addicts. I know of one case, some years ago, of a pregnant woman who, because of her history of addiction, was refused admission to four hospitals for delivery of her child.

Why expect more of the legislatures than this? It is not, mind you, that they are ignorant of the problem. Norm Eddy and others have seen to it that they are not. I myself have engaged in lobbying in Albany for legislation regarding narcotics and have testified before the President's Committee on Narcotics, along with hosts of others, including eminent medical authorities, social workers, clergy, judges, and law enforcement officers. The legislators know the facts. They all know the recommendations of those, many of them experts, who have been close to this issue. But expect no action from them. There is no great public interest and no significant political advantage accruing to legislative action in this field. Addicts aren't voters! Those who advocate their cause have little influence in terms of votes or campaign contributions. Legislatures in American society today, both local and national, respond not to social and public needs, but to economic and political pressures. All the addicts have on their side is their need.

Even where there is some public interest and political mileage for legislators in an issue, the underrepresentation and substantial disenfranchisement of the poor means that legislation is often enacted which fails woefully to meet the problems which it is intended to solve.

Consider, for example, urban redevelopment through private investment. The federal government is authorized by law to very substantially subsidize slum clearance undertaken by private capital. The local authority condemns a blighted area; it is transferred to a private developer who, with the subsidy and his own investment, builds a housing project. An admirable scheme. It clears the slums, encourages private enterprise, reduces federal spending for housing. The only trouble is that it does not seem to work out quite so neatly. The projects of this sort which I have seen—not only in New York, but in the south side of Chicago, in Washington, and elsewhere—are, for the most part, ones in which slums have been demolished and the occupants dispossessed. However, much of the new housing constructed has been luxury, semiluxury and middle-income units beyond the means of the former situs residents. The effect has been to reduce the total area of the slums, and at the same time, force those who cannot afford the new housing back into the constricting area of slums, thus congesting them all the more.

Rent control legislation in New York City, meanwhile, still applies to most slum dwellings. The law is, in effect, a continuation of the original rent control legislation of the Second World War. It has not been overhauled in its fundamental provisions since that time and its applicability has been gradually whittled down, since, through urban renewal, private renovation of housing, and new construction replacing old properties, rental units can be decontrolled. Complete abolition of rent control in New York is a perennial political objective of real estate investors and speculators. At the same time, the continued retention of rent control on unrenovated or unreplaced housing, which dates back to the original enactment of rent control, is a stock issue by which the political candidates appeal for the votes of liberals among the middle and upper classes. Hardly anyone bothers to inquire of the poor who live in rent-controlled slums how the law, supposedly retained for their benefit, actually works. If such inquiries were made, it would be found that in all too many instances the law works against the economic welfare of such tenants. One provision of the law authorizes automatic rent increases each time a tenancy changes. With the influx of Puerto Ricans to New York City since the end of the war, together with the movement of those dispossessed by urban renewal projects, many tenements have had numerous changes of tenancy in the past decade and a half. With each change, the rent increases. In consequence, one can find many families living in appallingly tiny, crowded, rodent- and vermin-infested slum dwellings and paying astronomical rentals in terms of what they receive. Even higher rents for housing outside the ghetto and discrimination in housing in the outer city prevent such families from moving elsewhere. In some instances it may, in fact, be more profitable for a landlord to hold onto his slum properties, deliberately not renovating them and thus not decontrolling them, because he can thus secure a wider profit margin with these grossly inflated, but entirely legal, controlled rents. In short, the present rent control law, in many instances at least, represents an economic bonanza for the landlord, and works an economic hardship for the tenants—it achieves the opposite result from what, it may be presumed, was legislatively intended and from what the politicans boast to the voters of liberal disposition outside the slums its social purpose is.

There is a recurrent political and legislative controversy in the urban sectors of the country with regard to public welfare assistance. One of the stock arguments of those who would abolish or radically curtail such programs is that they tend to encourage idleness, diminish individual initiative, and waste public funds. I have dealt with scores and scores of people who receive public assistance—most frequently in cases where there are minor children, often where there is no employed or employable father or other adult in the household. In all of these I have encountered only a handful of freeloaders. Most, to an overwhelming extent, have been people who want to work but who live in a society which has provided for them, sometimes just because of their race, no adequate educational opportunity to acquire working skills. Even where some education has been provided, either no jobs are to be had, or the jobs are marginal, providing such low income that welfare supplements were required to feed and clothe the children. There is every likelihood that the ranks of those on welfare will greatly increase, especially among Negroes and Puerto Ricans displaced even from menial jobs by automation. How can the affluent white society complain when these people apply for relief? That same society has failed almost utterly to make any provisions for the retraining and placement of these citizens in self-supporting occupations.

Meanwhile, let those who are so passionate in their concern for the dignity of the individual and the rights of the person give some attention to the grotesque invasions of privacy practiced in the supervision of the welfare program in the city. Welfare families are not only subject to investigation as to the legitimacy of their application and need, but also to visits and searches in their homes in the middle of the night by zealous welfare investigators seeking to find evidence of cheating or deception on the part of welfare recipients. I had one case in which an investigator climbed a tree at two o'clock in the morning in order to perch there and spy into the window of a project apartment of a welfare family, waiting to see or hear something that could be used against the family to disqualify them from further assistance.

Excesses in the welfare program there surely are—the ones that I have seen are those of gross invasions of privacy and abuses of discretion in administrative surveillance and investigation of welfare recipients. Those who want to reduce the costs of welfare can begin by (1) instituting programs, both private and public, which will educate, prepare, and place people in jobs; and (2) pruning the budget for the welfare "police."

One of the dilemmas that some slum families face is that the jobs open to them pay less than they are legally entitled to receive from welfare for the care of their families. This has been notoriously the case with hospital workers in private institutions related to churches or charitable agencies. Such institutions, until recently, were exempted by law in New York State from the provisions of the Labor Relations Act pertaining to collective bargaining with a union representing a majority of the workers.

The fact that there was no collective bargaining in such hospitals has meant that they have paid their nonprofessional hospital employees whatever they have been willing to pay. Some years ago a campaign to organize such hospital workers was initiated by Local 1199 of the Hospital and Pharmaceutical Workers Union. There was a long and terrific struggle before a bill finally was enacted which secured for these workers collective bargaining rights and opened the way for some chance at a decent and livable wage.

The Governor, though professing the usual sympathies for poor people, was frank to say, early in the fight for the bill, that he would not support it until it was clear that there were votes for him to be gained in supporting it. Several strikes occurred during the struggle for enactment of the legislation. Most everyone agreed that strikes in hospitals jeopardize public health, and the union was prepared to agree to a compulsory arbitration clause in the legislation. This angered most of the rest of the union movement, and caused the official opposition to the bill by the State AFL–CIO. The two other main elements of opposition were the hospital administrations, who, with rapidly rising medical costs, were not in a mood to agree to legislation that would undoubtedly lead to increased costs for wages. No one seemed concerned as to whether hospital deficits should be partly absorbed by maintaining the lowest possible pay to hospital workers who were, of all elements in society, least able economically to bear the burden. I was drawn into the fight for the hospital workers' bill largely because a good many of my neighbors and clients were hospital workers and I knew of their situation, and also because the other chief opposition to the legislation came from the churches with affiliated hospitals. One of the most bitter strikes, early in the struggle, had been at a Jewish hospital. The Roman Catholic authorities, with more hospitals under their auspices than any other faith, were determined in their opposition. Most Protestant-related institutions were also opposed, on the costs issue, though, as I found out, few at that time appreciated the burdens of their own employees due to their pitiful wages. Perhaps the strategy was that if some of the leading Protestant ecclesiastics could be persuaded to endorse the bill, this would help to neutralize the opposition of other religious authorities. Meanwhile, Local 1199 attempted to cope with the opposition from other unions to compulsory arbitration, while a citizens' group, mainly of Harlem leaders, sought to impress the Governor and the legislative leadership that it was politically beneficial to schedule the bill for adoption. The increasing eruption of the broader civil rights movement finally made the work of the latter citizens' committee persuasive to the politicians (though in this, let it be recorded, they were greatly helped by the Republican Speaker of the Assembly, Joseph Carlino, who from an early date had had the foresight and courage to support the bill in spite of the formidable opposition). Local 1199 fought militantly and passionately for the bill, without help from other unions, in a way reminiscent of some of the pioneer struggles for recognition in the early days of the American labor movement. They were aided in this by the court, probably inadvertently, when a judge cited and jailed the leader of the union, Leon Davis, for contempt of court for picketing, despite an injunction one of the hospitals had secured against such action. Legally, the court's decision is, in my own view as a lawyer, open to grave question. Practically, it appeared to be an excessive penalty, even if legally defensible, and oppressive to these workers. In consequence, there was an avalanche of publicity which finally brought the whole matter to the attention and conscience of the general public, and which probably was the decisive event of the whole effort. After a lot of legwork and a lot of talk, both about hospital workers and the Christian faith, several ranking Protestant ecclesiastics publicly endorsed the bill, as did certain church agencies, and also a large number of Protestant hospital chaplains. Even with these break-throughs, the battle was nip and tuck until the end. The bill enacted is not all that could be desired, but with this massive effort on several fronts, a step was taken to alleviate the situation of the hospital workers.

This little bridgehead does not, of course, change the slum homes to which so many hospital workers, like legions of other workers in the city, return every night. Nor does it alter the school situation or the problems of job retraining for displaced workers or the multitude of other problems that fester in the ghetto, of which, I fear, most of the outer city is oblivious. But it is a little bridgehead. As the present social revolution gains momentum, and if, as in this case, it has real support from both inside and outside the existing ghettos, and if somehow the cities are saved from violence (as doubtful as that now seems to be), then there will be bridges as well.

The Politics of Racism

A whole social order has to change, however, before there will be such a day. For one thing, in politics the quisling system must go. The political recognition which Negroes have so far received in New York—or the other great Northern cities—in *any* of the parties, including the parties that boast most of being liberal and concerned with civil rights—has been, in the multitude of cases, purchased by the surrender of their identity and integrity as Negroes. Prominent Negro politicians are regarded, with few exceptions, as servants of the old order, as "Uncle Toms," and for years have been secretly, but now openly, denounced as such by the restless, strident voices that can be heard in Harlem. One Negro, for instance, who for some years held high office in the city government was commonly called "the Black Italian"—a vulgar way to put it, I suppose, but it makes the point.

More recently, some incumbent white politicians, fearing that the time is at hand when Negroes will assume both title *and* power in city politics, fearfully and vehemently and repeatedly attack Negroes for trying to "take over" the city. Political prejudice against Negroes in New York is no longer mingled with the laughter and cursing in the back rooms of the political clubs, but now has the dignity it has so long had in the Deep South as grist for the speeches of white candidates.

Meanwhile the old-style Negro demagogues in politics, who have been enriched by their long and tacit collaboration with white politicians in suppressing the political rights and aspirations of Negroes with flamboyant diversions and cynical promises, are losing their hold in Harlem politics and preparing to flee the city with their loot, like Latin American potentates. They know that their era is overthrown.

Some old-line Negro politicians have been inadvertently given a new lease on their political lives, however, because of the intensity of racial feeling among both black and white people. Adam Clayton Powell has reigned for a long time as a Congressman and as minister of the largest Negro church in Harlem. He is not only a mixture of politician and preacher, but he has some of the aura of a matinee idol. In the days when almost the only famous Negroes in American society were boxers and entertainers, Adam was famous. Adam drove a foreign sports car. Adam went night-clubbing—at downtown clubs. Adam wore silk suits. Adam had escorted beautiful women. Adam raised hell in speeches. Adam went junketing to Europe. Adam became a very appealing symbol in Harlem. If he carried on a lot, if he lived extravagantly, if the gossip about him was all true—so what? Harlem forgave him all of that because at last somebody from Harlem—a Negro—was living it up the way the white folks do. That was the symbol of Adam, and in many ways it proved a more attractive symbol than, say, the dignity and accomplishments of Ralph Bunche.

Adam's day has lasted a long time, but a new and different and more responsible leadership among Negroes is emerging. The day of his kind of politics and leadership, providing a merely vicarious compensation for the people of Harlem, is essentially over. Yet Adam still lingers in power not only because of his own shrewdness, but because of coincidence and also the stupidity of others. His flaunting of a libel judgment against him, for example, enhances his appeal in a community in which there is deep hostility to the law. His seniority in the Congress has placed him in a strategic position to exploit the patronage angles of the war on poverty. Some years ago there was indication that Congressman Powell had intended to retire from politics. At that time he even resigned from his pulpit. Several prominent Harlem Negroes were considering candidates for his seat in the House of Representatives. But then Powell came under attack from white colleagues in the Congress about his trips abroad at government expense. Powell's response to this attack was that he was being criticized only because he is a Negro. His defense gained credibility when he produced verified records of the expenditures of several other Congressmen who had been abroad recently at taxpayers' expense. All of the other Congressmen were white; all had incurred significantly higher expenses. Promptly thereafter, Powell decided to run for re-election. Because those attacking him have mainly been self-serving white politicians, so far as I can ascertain, no other Negro will oppose him in the primary, not even those who most seriously question his approach to politics. His opponents in the Congress have succeeded, not in discrediting Powell, but in giving him a new lease on his political life.

The last years have brought to New York the so-called reform movement in the Democratic Party, but there have been few signs, so far as places like Harlem are concerned, of any substantial political change, either being promised or achieved. The reform movement tends merely to imitate the traditions and practices of the old-line Democratic machine. In one primary a few years ago, in which a reform candidate was contesting for a local nomination against the organization choice, some voters reported that the reform candidate had outbid the regular candidate in buying votes (the reform candidate was offering five dollars; the organization, only three). In another district nearby, during a voter registration period, some persons who were registered for the first time admitted that the reform candidate had supplied them with the answers to the literacy test. In some instances, too, reform Democrats have been just as loathe as old-line organizations either to nominate Negroes or Puerto Ricans for significant political or party offices or to welcome them into their policy-making forums. The complexion of the reform movement may be, and I think is, more democratic in some other parts of the city, but reform has not meant, in my observation, any great political emancipation for the people of Harlem and East Harlem, and this has served to deepen the cynicism of people there about politics. This, as much as anything, has provoked the advocacy among Northern urban Negroes of an all-Negro political party.

During one campaign year, approaches were made to me to be a candidate for a local office by some of those associated with the reform Democratic movement and also by some of the leaders of the Liberal Party in New York State. The latter—though a minority party—often is in a position to swing an election to a candidate of one of the major parties by giving that candidate its nomination. Initially, the overture came from the reform Democrats. I would contest the Democratic primary with the regular Democrat, and later it was thought fairly certain that the Liberal Party endorsement could also be obtained. Even if the primary were lost to the regular Democratic candidate, I would still then run on the Liberal Party line. I discussed the matter with a good many people in both the Democratic and Liberal parties, as well as with friends from the Harlem neighborhood and others, and participated in a number of caucuses. I decided that I would not run for office myself, but would try to persuade the reformers and the Liberals to support a Negro or a Puerto Rican candidate, since this section had never had such representation, despite the large numbers of Negro and Puerto Rican residents in the neighborhood. After several more caucuses, mainly with Negroes and Puerto Ricans from the district, a young Negro was agreed upon as the person who would be proposed to the Liberals and the reformers. By this time the organization candidate had been designated. As it happened, he had the same surname as the Negro who was our proposed candidate. That would add some interest and humor to the campaign, I recall thinking, and insofar as it might cause some confusion among voters, I felt that the confusion would accrue mainly to the benefit of our side.

Several of us then set about negotiating for the backing of the reform Democrats and the Liberals. The former rather quickly decided that the time had not yet come for so radical a step as a Negro candidate. They argued that it would arouse greater than ordinary opposition from the regular organization. So they refused their endorsement. Subsequently, the reformers endorsed a woman, who, if anything, elicited even greater opposition from the regular Democrats than a Negro would have, and whose candidacy was rendered ridiculous because of her absence in Europe on vacation during most of the primary campaign period.

Rejected—I forbear to speculate upon the real reasons for it—by the reformers, we persevered in negotiations with the Liberals. Generally, among the higher-echelon Liberal Party leaders we received encouragement, as we did from some of the union leaders who invariably support the Liberal Party. But each one attached the proviso to his endorsement that the proposed candidate would have to be cleared with the division chief of the party's staff who was in charge of Negro and Puerto Rican recruitment for the Liberals. A delegation was assembled and a summit conference held with this headquarters staff officer, who is a Puerto Rican. The endorsement of our proposed candidate was vetoed there.

As I look back upon it, such a veto was predictable, and we should probably have conducted our negotiations in a different, and less candid and direct, manner. In any case, it was clear that the staff of the party, at that time at least, in charge of recruitment of Negroes and Puerto Ricans was not about to endorse for office in a heavily Negro or Puerto Rican district a candidate who was not selected by and dependent upon the party staff. To accede to the nomination we proposed, that is, an outsider and newcomer, would have meant a dilution of the domain of the Negro-Puerto Rican staff section of the party. Especially if our candidate made a good showing, even though he did not win—and there was little chance of winning with Liberal support only—he would have laid claim to the Liberal Party leadership in the district from which he ran, which constituted about one-fourth of the total jurisdiction of the staff section in question. Why should they aid anyone in succeeding to any of their power?

Though we may have been naïve in our strategy in trying to secure the Liberal designation in this instance, the broader issue raised by this experience was the exclusionary effect of ethnic and racial departments within political parties. Such departments, although presumably conceived and designed to attract special groups of voters and candidates from various races and nationalities, tend, in actual fact, to discourage free entrance into the party structures. The manifest vested interest of those in charge of such departments in maintaining a personal control over those whom they recruit effectively obstructs participation in the parties.

The Liberal Party in New York is no different in this respect from the Republican and Democratic parties, both on state and national levels. Ethnic recruitment, as such, by the parties reduces rather than increases the ethnic diversity of the political parties.

Remembering the lesson in the Liberal Party incident, the strategy was altered during the first gubernatorial campaign of Nelson Rockefeller. By this time Harlem had become increasingly disenchanted both with regular and reform Democrats and with the Liberals as well, and the Rockefeller family's prior reputation and philanthrophy in aid of Negroes were a substantial asset to Nelson Rockefeller's first campaign. However, he persisted in a conventional campaign in Harlem, and it became clear that the advice he was receiving about the Harlem community was, to say the least, out-of-date and out-of-touch with the more militant mood then manifesting itself there. Somehow the news drifted back to the Rockefeller campaign headquarters that this was so and one day a call was received from an intermediary, indicating that Mr. Rockefeller was interested in meeting with some citizens of Harlem, regardless of party, to hear their views on the conditions and issues there to which his campaign might be addressed. A delegation to meet with Rockefeller was decided upon, made up of Negroes, Puerto Ricans, and white people. The delegation determined, however, that two conditions were to be required before they would be willing to meet with the candidate. One was that the meeting not be a perfunctory ceremony—an audience in which they would be ushered in, greeted, and ushered out. If he wanted to listen to their views, they were ready to meet with him, but they would need more than five or ten minutes. The other condition was that no one be present but the nominee. They knew that the nominee was relying for advice as to his campaign among Negroes and Puerto Ricans upon the same staff of Uncle Toms (or so many others regarded them) that other Republican candidates had relied upon for years. They were able enough people, but, as is characteristic of Uncle Toms, they had lost touch with Harlem, many had moved away, and also, understandably, they suffered from the instinct to preserve their own vested interests. The delegation had, I think, no personal or competitive hostility toward them—none were Republicans. They were concerned to discuss some issues openly and to inform the nominee as accurately as they were in a position to do, then let him return to his advisers on Negro and Puerto Rican affairs, listen also to them, and then do whatever he wished about his own campaign. At the same time, they did not think that they were free to be frank with the nominee unless they met with him privately.

The conference was arranged. About fifteen minutes before the appointed time the delegation gathered in the lobby of the hotel where the meeting was to be held. Shortly after they had all assembled, a message was received, expressing Mr. Rockefeller's regrets that the meeting could not be held under the conditions which had been set forth.

So be the politics of racism.

Poverty, Charity, and Mission

Meanwhile, there were other fronts which required attention besides the politics of the city and the practice of law in Harlem. I had come initially to Harlem as a member of the group ministry of the East Harlem Protestant Parish, out of concern for the mission of the Church to the poor and to those socially discriminated against in the city.

When I first moved to the neighborhood the parish was suffering from a terrific confusion as to the nature of the Church and the meaning and manner of the Church's task in a place such as Harlem. At the heart of these issues were some of the same matters which so divide the several churches outside of Harlem. They provoked deep divisions within the parish, particularly among the members of the group ministry, who, apart from myself and one other man, were clergymen.

Through its first years in the neighborhood the parish had become deeply conformed to the world. Conformity to the world is a temptation which assails the Church no less in the slums than in the suburbs. Conformity to the world exists whenever and wherever the Church regards its message and mission to be primarily determined by, or essentially dominated by, the ethos of secular life and the society which surrounds the Church.

The young ministers who had come out of Union Theological Seminary to found the East Harlem Protestant Parish were much tempted to such conformity. They had seen the Protestant churches abandon the inner city, both physically and psychologically, and were aroused by this attachment and conformity of Protestantism to middle-class American society. They would bring the ministry of Protestantism back into the inner city and work there among the poor and the dispossessed. In doing so they were confronted with how the ministry could be exercised in the midst of the long-festering, complex, and, to them —since they were white middle- and upper-class people— unfamiliar social problems that characterize urban slum society. To these problems they brought two things—a hostility toward the conventional churches outside the slums, which caused them to think they had little or nothing to learn from the life of the Church outside East Harlem, and a sincere passion for social change and revolution, even, in East Harlem. These two emotions joined to underscore the view that before the Gospel could be preached and received by the people of the slums, the way for the Word had to be prepared by improving the education of the people, renovating their housing, finding jobs for them, clearing the streets of garbage and debris, challenging the political status quo, alleviating the narcotics problem, and by social action of all sorts. When some of these issues had been resolved, when the lives of the people were less burdened with poverty, discrimination, illiteracy, and ignorance, then the time would come to preach the Gospel and then the people, no longer so preoccupied with their afflictions, would be able to hear and embrace the Gospel. One of the earlier parish documents declares that the parish "is a group ministry of twelve men and women working at the neighborhood level to help people face and work on their problems." Ironically, in spite of their rejection of middle-class Protestantism, the group ministry initially seems to have seen its task as making the East Harlem neighborhood more nearly middle class! Such a prejudgment is marred by the same sort of confusion that beset many missionaries who, in the early days of American foreign missions, went to Africa, Latin America, and the Far East, and who thought that before the people indigenous to those places could understand

and receive the Word of God in Christ, they first had to
be Westernized.

One of the paradoxes is that, unlike the people to whom
the Western missionaries ventured, the American Negro
is not foreign to the traditions, culture, class ethos, and
social mores of American society. All these are his own
inheritance. The American Negro, in other words, is an
American—and he has been such for as long or longer
than any other ethnic group in the United States. What
he remembers is American, not African. What he remembers is, however, an American ethos, from which he has
been deliberately excluded. What he remembers is that
he has been forcibly separated from those things which
are as much his own as any other American's. What he
remembers are the very promises of the American Revolution—human dignity and equal treatment, fair representation and the opportunity to be politically free, the right
to education and employment and a decent place to live
and raise his children. No one has to instill these ideas
and aspirations in American Negroes. They have inherited
and remember them, despite three hundred years of slavery and segregation. They honor them by enduring their
breach. They honor them more than most other Americans.

In any event, the preaching and service of the Gospel
do not depend upon any special social change, ideation-
ally or in any other way. The Gospel does not even depend upon the American way of life, either in its integrity
or its breach.

I am as much in favor of social change in the urban
ghettos as the next man, perhaps more (though I am by
no means persuaded that the standard of social improvement should be that of the great American bourgeoisie),
but the message and mission of the Church in the world
never depend upon the specific physical, political, cultural,
social, economic, or even psychological situations in which

the Church, or the people of the Church as missionaries, find themselves. If the Gospel is so contingent as that, it is no universal Gospel. If the Gospel is so fragile that it may not be welcomed by a man who, say, is hungry, unless he first be fed, then this is no Gospel with any saving power, this is no Word of God which has authority over the power of death. The Gospel, if it represents the power of God unto salvation, is a Word which is exactly addressed to men in this world in their destitution and hunger and sickness and travail and captivity and perishing, in a way which may be heard and embraced by men in any of these, or in any other, afflictions. That is, by the way, the original portrait and report of Christian witness in the world, in the days of the Acts of the Apostles.

The Church is much tempted by conformity to the world, by accommodating the message and mission to the particular society in which the Church happens to be, in the slums and in the suburbs, instead of honoring the integrity of the Gospel for all societies and for all sorts and conditions of men in all times and places. This temptation beguiled the group ministry of the East Harlem Protestant Parish. They plunged into all sorts of social work and social action—narcotics, politics, neighborhood improvement, education, housing, and the rest. They instituted therapy and counseling for addicts, engaged in voter registration, lobbied for new playgrounds, organized P.T.A.s, complained about slum landlords, and, generally, made themselves a nuisance to those in power in the neighborhood. It was, in many ways, an admirable, if idealistic, and, in Christian terms, naïve effort. But they neglected and postponed the proclamation and celebration of the Gospel in East Harlem. In the congregations of the parish, the Bible was closed; in the group ministry there was even scorn for the Bible as a means through which the Word of God is communicated in contemporary society. The liturgical life of the congregations grew erratic and fortuitous, depending upon the personality and whim, even, of the minister presiding at the time. There was no concord or confession of the faith among either the group ministry or the lay people; there was a radical substitution of conventional charity for the mission of the Church. The parish—and especially the group ministry—was becoming dependent, in its *raison d'être,* upon its "good works," rather than upon the Gospel, as such, for its justification.

In such circumstances, the hostility of the group ministry toward the Church outside East Harlem, and, indeed, toward other churches within East Harlem unaffiliated with the parish—such as the Chambers Memorial Baptist Church or St. Edward the Martyr or The Church of the Good Neighbor or the Roman Catholic Churches thereabouts—became more arrogant and proud. Not long after I had come to East Harlem, one of the clergy in the group ministry blandly explained that the Church outside East Harlem was dead and that the East Harlem Protestant Parish represented the "New Jerusalem"—to quote his exact words—of American Protestantism, the example through which American Protestantism would be purified and renewed. The calling of the parish, he assured me, was to be the norm, in all essential realms of the Church's life, for the whole Church in American society. I recall replying, in more strenuous language than I will use here, that he was mistaken and that part of the reason he was mistaken in this ambition for the parish was contained in his manifest ignorance, along with others (though not all in the group ministry), about the life of the Church outside East Harlem. For the fact was that very few of the clergy of the parish at this time had had any experience in the Church, apart from their special experience in East Harlem itself. Of the twenty or so members of the group ministry on the scene when I first came to the neighborhood and to the parish, only five of us—George Todd,

Melvin Schoonover, Geoffrey Ainger, Donald De Young, and myself—had had any significant involvement in the life of the Church outside East Harlem, especially in any ecumenical sense.

The dangerous aspects of the parish's attitude were not just its wholesale rejection of the Church outside East Harlem, not even its conviction that mission is dependent upon and follows charity. More important, the group ministry was intent on conformity to the world and too easily disposed to think of itself as the model of the Church in American society. Members of the group ministry were filled with stereotyped opinions about the condition of the Church outside the inner city, but, except for a few of us, none of them had ever lived in the Church outside or had any first-hand knowledge of any church other than the parish.

At this stage in the parish's struggle to survive and to become a responsible member of the Church, the parish —and specifically the group ministry—was in danger of becoming sectarian, in danger of becoming so conformed to their environment and so dominated by it that the understanding of the Church which was asserted had become essentially joined to the sort of place in the world in which the parish was established. The Church could be the Church, to put it plainly, only in the slums. That is sectarianism, no less than it is where a church is established on grounds of class or race or language or any other secular criteria.

But this is not only sectarianism, it is romanticism. East Harlem is a frontier of the Church, but it is no more a frontier of the Church than the university or suburbia or anywhere else. Fanfare and special pleading and self-serving propaganda about the inner city ministry are both misleading and obscene. East Harlem, the earlier emphasis of the parish there notwithstanding, is in itself no more a frontier than any other place in the world. A frontier is wherever the Church trusts the Gospel in the Gospel's inherent relevance to the whole of life in this world. A frontier is wherever the Church exercises the freedom which God gives the Church to share the burden of any man, in order to make known how Christ bears all burdens of every man everywhere and in all times.

The sectarianism of the parish at this period was perhaps particularly sensitive to my own presence in the group ministry because I am an Episcopalian, and before coming to the parish, I had had a certain experience not only within the Anglican Communion, but in the ecumenical movement, especially in the World's Student Christian Federation and in the World Council of Churches. From that background and experience I knew something of the ministry of the Church outside East Harlem and, frankly, I was not impressed with the ready assurances that the East Harlem Protestant Parish represented the prototype of the renewal of the Church in the world, as much as I instinctively admired the social concern of the members of the group ministry. Even before affiliating with the parish, I had not hesitated to be critical of my own denomination or of the churches at large. Indeed, on the basis of my own involvement in the Church outside of East Harlem, and in view of the lack of significant involvement in or commitment to the Church outside by most, save a few, members of the group ministry, I felt authorized to say within the group ministry that not only were they not the image of the "new Jerusalem" and more than likely were building a new sect, based upon their location in and concern for the inner city, but they were guilty of the same conformity to the world which characterizes the churches and sects that take their identity and task from their place and status in the suburbs or elsewhere.

As time went on, the controversy about the nature of the Church and about the mission of the Church became gravely intensified within the group ministry, and, over a period of months, it focused upon two principal issues, although there were many ancillary matters which were also involved from time to time.

The first was centered upon the significance of the Bible for Christian people and for the life of the Church. Some of the members of the group ministry were appallingly diffident toward the Bible; and those who were the most self-serious about the analysis of culture and society were most often the dilettantes in Bible study. Those professing condolence for people showed mostly indolence for the Bible. Apparently, some of the clergy felt that Bible study was unnecessary, since they had already learned all they needed to of the Bible in seminary.

To some others in the group ministry—and to myself—this seemed astonishing in the extreme, especially among Protestants who might be expected to recall that, historically, Protestants have been a people of the Word of God in the Bible. Surely, intimacy with the Word of God in the Bible, reliance upon the Word of God in the Bible, is a characteristic of the ordinary practice of the Christian life, it seemed to those of us who urged that the group ministry and the people of the congregations engage in some corporate Bible study each week. After much controversy about the matter, it was decided that the group would spend an hour or so in Bible study just before the regular weekly staff meetings. It was often an erratic, sparsely attended—or attended to—exercise, but it exposed the fundamental disunity within the group ministry as to the content of the Christian faith and the nature of the Church's life and work. In this Bible study, the minds of some were filled with notions of truth, ideas of good, with interesting hypotheses, strong sentiments, and current events—and these things were actually asserted to test the Word of God. But few seemed ready just to *listen* to the Word of God in the Bible, to ask: What *is* the Word of

God? Now, later, much later, after many struggles and
both indifference and resistance, with the counsel and
nurture of such visitors to the parish as Suzanne de
Dietrich, Hendrik Kraemer, and others, the Bible has
been acknowledged as central in the life of the Church
and, hence, of this parish—but only after much agony.

At the heart of the conflict and disunity regarding the
place of the Bible in the Church—as in many other
churches outside Harlem—was a fundamental misapprehension about what the Bible is. I have no inclination
toward Biblical literalism, but neither do I think that the
Bible can be neglected, as the liberal Protestants fondly do,
save for the teachings of Jesus. I am no Biblical scholar,
either, but I affirm the necessity for the most rigorous
work of textual criticism and the like. I do not become
greatly distressed by "demythologizing" the Bible unless
it is used as an excuse for banishing the Bible from contemporary life. None of these approaches to the Bible
essentially affects the reliance upon the Bible of the ordinary Christian as a particular means through which the
Word of God is uttered and may be heard by men no less
today than in the earlier days of the Christian people. In
other words, and without denigrating an appropriate place
for Biblical scholarship and criticism, the characteristic
approach to the Bible of the Christian is confessional.
The Christian confronts the Bible in the expectancy that
it is in and through the testimony of the Bible of God's
presence and action in the common life of the world that
he will behold the Word of God as such, that he will hear
the Word of God in the objectivity, integrity, and serenity
of God's own witness to Himself in this history, that he
will confront the *living* Word. The Word of God, in this
sense, mediated through the narrative, history, praise,
testimony, and exhortation of the Bible, lives by God's
own initiative and generosity in this world, apart from
whether or not men listen to God's Word, apart from hu-

man wisdom and scholarship, apart from tampering with or manipulation of the Bible, apart from the interesting and even sometimes true views and opinions of men, apart from any hardness of heart. The Word of God, in this sense, which is mediated in and through the Bible, is the very same Word of God in which all life in the whole of creation originates, the same Word embodied and exposed in Jesus Christ, the same Word by which the world is judged and in which the world is fulfilled, the same Word of God present and active in the world in the present day and in each and every event and transaction of everyday life in the world. Thus, when the Christian turns to the Bible in a confessional sense, he does so in the expectancy of discerning the same Word of God with which he is confronted in his involvement each day in the common life of the world. And in his experience of the Word of God in the Bible, on one hand, and in common life, on the other hand, each is confirmed by the other. This is the case, not because a man is especially learned or wise or even diligent, but because the Word of God is indeed a living Word whose vitality is no less to be beheld and enjoyed in ordinary life today than in the saga of the Word of God in the history of the people Israel, in the Gospels of Christ's ministry, in the birth and beginnings of the Church, in the acts and testimonies of the first apostles and evangelists known to us through the Bible.

I count the diffidence toward the Bible in the group ministry, accompanied as it was by the neglect of reliance upon the Bible in preaching in the parish's congregations and in the liturgical practices of these congregations, as the reason for the gross misapprehension about theology in the group ministry in the days of which I speak. Somehow the parish clergy had come to think that theology is the theory of the Christian faith which, once comprehended and accepted, is to be applied and executed in practical action in the world. That is why, I suppose, that the honor given by some of us to the Bible as mediator of the living Word of God still at work in this world was unwelcome and received with such vigorous hostility by our colleagues in the group ministry. The role of man would be so much more important if he did not always have to watch for the presence and initiative of the Word of God in history. If this Word was not still active, God would be remote—if not, in fact, dead. Then, men could choose to justify themselves by their own words, and one could take or leave the Bible, as well as the inherited testimony of earlier Christians, according to one's own individual ethics or speculations. Carried to its logical extreme, such a position implies atheism. Although there are many sincere and honorable men who are atheists, there is no excuse for such men to masquerade as Christians.

The neglect, and in some instances outright suppression, of the Bible as a mediator of the Word of God gravely influenced the ministry of the parish in its day-to-day relations to the neighborhood around it. It meant, for one thing, a failure to respect the office of the laity in the parish congregations. For all practical purposes, they were excluded from the government of the parish— they had no authority in the calling of their own ministers, in determining the service of the parish to the community, in supporting the parish's ministry in a significant way; they were, in short, appendices of the group ministry, dependent upon the leadership and resources of the ecclesiastical authorities, objects of the ministry rather than participants in the total ministry of the Church in East Harlem. As has happened before, in the Church of Rome as well as in the churches of Protestantism, the group ministry at this time was becoming so overinstitutionalized, so large, so aggressive, and so self-contained that it took upon itself the prerogatives of a congregation. The group ministry not only met with great frequency—apart from the congregations—to make policy, raise and spend funds, plan tactics and the like, but it also met often, including Sunday mornings, to worship separately from the congregations. In practice, the esoteric life of the group ministry had become one which really claimed that the group ministry constituted the community of the faithful in this neighborhood, and that the people who were baptized and had been made members of the several congregations of the parish were consigned to some derivative and peripheral status in the ministry of the Church in East Harlem. The paradox of the group ministry, as it actually operated then, was that the group ministry itself was the chief and constant threat to the emergence of vital congregations among the people of East Harlem, while, at the same time, the emergence of some congregations in East Harlem was the most substantial threat to the group ministry as a congregation and as a paternalistic ecclesiastical institution.

The slothfulness of the group ministry in confronting such issues as these—the place of the Bible in the Church and the adjacent issues of preaching and liturgy and action in society, plus the office of the laity and its relationship to the ecclesiastical ministry—provoked some of us to leave the group ministry after a while. I resigned about fifteen months after first coming to the neighborhood, but decided to stay in East Harlem, living and working as a lawyer on my own thereafter, and so remained until 1962. My resignation, let it be said, by no means terminated communication or collaboration with the people—both lay and clergy—of the parish on specific issues concerning both the church and society, but, I trust, the decision permitted both the group ministry and myself to persevere in the work which each felt called to do in East Harlem, in society at large, and in the ministry of the Church.

Since that time it appears that there have been significant changes in the parish, among others the admission of the laity to a significant voice in the affairs of the parish and also a serious renewal in the parish in the recognition of the uniqueness of the Bible as an evidence and honoring of the Word of God in the world.

As I recall upon these controversies, what they amounted to were reflections of the differences within American Protestantism at large as to the meaning of God's concern for and presence in this world. From my own vantage point and experience on that issue, the Christian faith is not about some god who is an abstract presence somewhere else, but about the living presence of God here and now, in this world, in *exactly* this world, as men know it and touch it and smell it and live and work in it. That is why, incidentally, all the well-meant talk of "making the gospel relevant" to the life of the world is false and vulgar. It secretly assumes that God is a stranger among us, who has to be introduced to us and to our anxieties and triumphs and issues and efforts. The meaning of Jesus Christ is that the Word of God is addressed to men, to *all* men, in the very events and relationships, any and every one of them, which constitute our existence in this world. That is the theology of the Incarnation.

The Word of God is present among the poor as well as among all others, and what I have called earlier the piety of the poor conceals the Word of God. The piety of the poor is prophetic: In a funny, distorted, ambiguous way it anticipates the Gospel. This is confirmed every day in East Harlem. There is a boy in the neighborhood, for instance, who is addicted to narcotics and whom I have defended in some of his troubles with the law. He used to stop in often on Saturday mornings to shave and wash up, after having spent most of the week on the streets. He has been addicted for a long time. His father threw him out about three years ago, when he was first arrested. He has contrived so many stories to induce clergy and social workers to give him money to support his habit that he is no longer believed when he asks for help. His addiction is heavy enough and has been prolonged enough so that he now shows symptoms of other trouble—his health is broken by years of undernourishment and insufficient sleep. He is dirty, ignorant, arrogant, dishonest, unemployable, broken, unreliable, ugly, rejected, alone. And he knows it. He knows at last that he has nothing to commend himself to another human being. He has nothing to offer. There is nothing about him that permits the love of another person for him. He is unlovable. Yet it is exactly in his own confession that he does not deserve the love of another that he represents all the rest of us. For none of us is different from him in this regard. We are *all* unlovable. More than that, the action of this boy's life points beyond itself, it points to the Gospel, to God who loves us though we hate Him, who loves us though we do not satisfy His love, who loves us though we do not please Him, who loves us not for our sake but for His own sake, who loves us freely, who accepts us though we have nothing acceptable to offer Him. Hidden in the obnoxious existence of this boy is the scandalous secret of the Word of God. [Stop | Tom]

It is, after all, in Hell—in that estate where the presence of death is militant and pervasive—that the triumph of God over death in Jesus Christ is decisive and manifest.

The Word of God is secretly present in the life of the poor, as in the life of the whole world, but most of the poor do not know the Word of God. These two facts constitute the dialectic of the Church's mission among the poor. All that is required for the mission of the Church in Harlem is there already, save one thing: the presence of the community which has and exercises the power to discern the presence of the Word of God in the ordinary life of the poor as it is lived every day. What is requisite to mission, to the exposure of God's Word within the precarious and perishing existence of poverty, is the congregation which relies on and celebrates the resurrection. That which is essential for mission is confession of the faith—immediately, notoriously, and in whatever terms or symbols or actions are indigenous to the moment and place.

The characteristic of the life of God which the Church needs most to recall nowadays, I think, is how absurdly simple His action in the world already makes our witness to Him in the world.

The churches have been beset by a false notion of charity. They have supposed that the inner city must become much more like the outer city before the Gospel can be heard. They have thought that mission follows charity. They have favored crusades and abandoned mission. I am all for changing the face of Harlem, but the mission of the Church depends not on social reformation in the neighborhood, as desperately as that is needed, but upon the presence of the Word of God in the society of the poor as it is right now. If the mere Gospel is not a whole salvation for the most afflicted men, it is no comfort to other men in less affliction. Mission does *not* follow charity; faith does *not* follow works, either for donor or recipient. On the contrary, mission is *itself* the only charity which Christians have to offer the poor, the only work which Christians have to do.

The premise of most urban church work, it seems, is that in order for the Church to minister among the poor, the church has to be rich, that is, to have specially trained personnel, huge funds and many facilities, rummage to distribute, and a whole battery of social services. Just the opposite is the case. The Church must be free to be poor in order to minister among the poor. The Church must trust the Gospel enough to come among the poor with nothing to offer the poor except the Gospel, except the power to apprehend and the courage to reveal the Word of God as it is already mediated in the life of the poor.

When the Church has the freedom itself to be poor among the poor, it will know how to use what riches it has. When the Church has that freedom, it will be a missionary people again in all the world.

Chapter Four
PREMONITION

On one of those steaming, stinking, stifling nights that summer brings to Harlem tenements, I had a dream:

In the dream, I was walking in Harlem on 125th Street, in broad daylight. I seemed to be the only white man in sight. The passers-by stared at me, ruefully. Then two Negroes stopped me and asked for a light. While I searched my pockets for a match, one of them sank a knife into my belly. I fell. I bled. After a while, I died.

I woke quickly.
I felt my stomach; there wasn't any blood.
I smoked a cigarette and thought about the dream:

The assault in the dream seemed unprovoked and vicious. The death in the dream seemed useless and, therefore, all the more expensive. The victim in the dream seemed innocent of offense against those who murdered him. Except, the victim was a white man. The victim was murdered by the black men because he was a white man. The murder was retribution. The motive was revenge.
No white man is innocent.
I am not innocent.

Then I cried.

Deception is more humiliating than rejection. Exploitation is more inhuman than exclusion. Indifference is more embittering than open hostility. Condescension is more provocative than hate.

The estrangement of the races in the North is more volatile, more apt to explode into violence, as far as I can discern, than is the segregation of the races in the South. The alienation of the races in New York City or Chicago may turn out to be more calamitous than whatever happens in Jackson or in Birmingham. For Negroes in the urban North, revenge may seem sweeter than equality, and violence more decisive than patience, and both more honorable than the tolerance of further appeasements and postponements.

Of course, I say this out of my own experience in New York—in Harlem—and from a good deal of contact with the people of the ghettos of some of the other Northern cities—Chicago, Boston, and Detroit, especially. But I assert it also in the perspective of some exposure to and experience in the South. During the years I lived and worked in Harlem I had occasion to visit the South a good many times. Sometimes, in Mississippi and in Louisiana, the Southern visits involved legal cases, but there were also trips to Georgia, South Carolina, Virginia, Florida, and Arkansas, to lecture at law schools and colleges and to visit some of the churches of the South. There were opportunities to give legal counsel to those involved in the sit-ins and Freedom Rides and other demonstrations, both in the South and the North.

Indeed, I myself was involved in what must have been one of the original sit-ins—back in 1943—when I was in college in Maine. Some of us had observed that Negroes were not served at a certain hotel and that discrimination existed and was practiced in some other public accommodations, although it must be said that the issue was hardly noticed publicly in Maine because there were comparatively few Negroes in the state. There was, however, discrimination in some places against French Canadians who had migrated to Maine. A bill was introduced into the legislature that condemned racial or ethnic discrimination, and that sought to establish a commission against discrimination. Several of us were working for the bill's enactment. One day the legislator who had sponsored the measure, a man of French extraction, came to see us to report that the legislation had almost no chance to pass, since there was so little public interest in the issue. After long discussion, it was decided that three of us would go with a Negro to the hotel which barred Negroes and ask to be served. It was arranged in advance that the legislator would be dining in the same hotel that evening and would have with him a newspaperman. The expectation was that we would ask to be served, and, as had been the custom in the hotel, be refused. We would protest, and the legislator, having noticed the incident, would intervene in our behalf while the newspaperman took photographs and got a story. The publicity of the incident was supposed to enhance the prospects for the passage of the bill. At the appointed hour, our party arrived at the hotel and went into the dining room. The senator and the reporter were halfway through their entrées. After we had been sitting at the table for several minutes, we noticed that the waiter had gone to speak to the manager. We could not hear their conversation, but soon the waiter came and asked to take our order. We had to order something of course. Ironically, we had already eaten at the college, so sure we were that the hotel would not serve us. Among the four of us we had only about five dollars, so the unfortunate senator ended up paying the check—for our second dinner of the evening! That was the result achieved in this pioneer sit-in.

It is against the background not only of Harlem, but of a bit broader involvement than that, that I conclude that the decisive front in the racial crisis in America is the urban North, and not the South. I have immense admiration for the restraint, dignity, and resourcefulness of the civil rights movement in the South, but the case remains that the immediate and stated objectives of that movement in the Southern jurisdictions are goals that have already been substantially achieved in the Northern cities, at least so far as court decisions and legislation are concerned, and also, to a significant degree, so far as integration in public transportation, hotels, restaurants, and the like is concerned. These things were attained in the North for the most part in the years after the Second World War, and what is to be seen, when one looks now at the Northern city, is what happens after these legal rights and remedies, which the Southern demonstrations seek to win, have been won. The Northern city, in other words, is setting the precedent for what is in store for the Southern cities, once the legal struggle to vindicate the civil rights of Negroes has been concluded. And if, in the days that lie immediately ahead, the relations between the races are not somehow resolved peacefully, then the whole nation is in for an ominous and dreadful holocaust.

Let no man take comfort in the racial troubles of the Northern cities, least of all any white man from the South, any more than any white Northerner can appease his conscience or rationalize his indifference by the racial strife in the South. No man is made innocent by the mere culpability of another man.

The Lost Frontier

Harlem had considered itself for a long time to be the pioneer Negro community, not only in the United States, but in the world. That seems a not unjustified pride. After all, New York City had been the place where the great succession of peoples of different tongues, nations, religions, and customs had come and found—albeit after patience and travail—mutual accommodation, a general acceptance, and a share in the prosperity, culture, political power, and common life of the city. New York City represented the hospitality of American democracy to each man and to all men. Surely the American Negro migrating from the South, and the West Indian Negro immigrating to the continent could find here, if anywhere, welcome, opportunity, dignity, and hope. Surely the Negroes of New York would become and be here the pioneers of their race, an example and encouragement and enhancement to all Negroes everywhere.

This pioneer psychology in Harlem was fed for years by the accumulation of civil rights laws and statutory disclaimers of racial discrimination, by the ceremonial use of Negroes in public affairs, by the praise of social equality for Negroes heard in the churches downtown, by the integration—although here it was from the outset the most obvious economic necessity—of public transportation and accommodations, by the gradual, if begrudged, inroads of Negroes into the lower echelons of public and quasi-public employment, by the notoriety that some few Negroes achieved in white society, particularly in athletics and entertainment.

Harlem was the leader, so long as the African nations remained largely colonial. Harlem was the pioneer, so long as the South remained segregated.

But now, under the impact of the events in Africa—the emergence of the new nations there and the increasingly decisive power of Africans in the United Nations—and with the disruption and accelerating disintegration of Southern segregation, Harlem frets over its destiny. Harlem wonders whether it has lost its pioneer initiative, and suspects that every achievement of Negroes in New York City and every opportunity of Negroes in New York City is illusory or fraudulent or guileful.

No wonder.

A few years ago, legislation was enacted in New York City barring discrimination in private multiple-dwelling units, a law much celebrated by the local politicians as a milestone for Negroes and other so-called minority groups in the city. Yet few Negroes look for housing outside of Harlem without encountering discrimination, in one guise or another. And even where the discriminating circumstances are such as to legally justify filing a complaint, the procedure for administration of the law is so cumbersome as to be of practical consequence in only a handful of cases.

The new construction and renovation of housing in New York have been an efficient instrument of segregation. The East Side of Manhattan, for instance, from Yorkville to Gramercy Park, is more effectually segregated today than it was fifteen years ago because the vast reconstruction of that sector of the city has made the rental or purchase of housing beyond the means of most Harlem Negroes. Yet, at the same time, I have been offered an apartment in Yorkville "for pretty much whatever you want to pay" by a landlord who "wants to keep the building white."

And if a Negro family wants to move out of Harlem and to Queens, say, and purchase a house there, they will find that the banks are helping to resist such moves by charging both the seller and the buyer "placing fees" in order to merely receive a mortgage application. Insofar as Negroes disperse in the city, both the Negroes and those willing to sell housing to Negroes have to pay a penalty for it.

The effect of factors such as these, despite the legislative denunciations of discrimination, is to induce the formation of new ghettos for Negroes in the places in the Bronx or Queens or Brooklyn or Beacon or Newburgh to which Negroes move from the Harlem ghetto. As the Negro population increases, new Harlems are spawned, which suffer the same isolation from the rest of the city that the old Harlem has known for more than half a century.

Housing is crucial, of course, because of the vitality of neighborhood life and the importance of neighborhood institutions in the city. If housing is segregated, then there will also be, and is, *de facto* segregation of schools, hospitals, political clubs, taverns, stores, and churches, even without other considerations that favor segregation in education, religion, politics, and the like.

Where slums have been displaced by public housing projects in areas like Harlem, the people have often been exploited by private businessmen who take advantage of the ignorance of people with regard to their rights. One of the common frauds is the furniture dealer who visits a family which has been accepted for public housing, to inform them that a prerequisite for moving into their new apartment is that they have new furniture. Such transactions typically result in the commitment of the family to a heavily mortgaged purchase of furniture of indifferent or inferior quality, with such small installment payments that they pay many times over the true value of the goods and are lucky if the furniture lasts as long as the payments. Of course, default in the payments entitles the seller to repossess the property.

Ironically, many of these sales based upon misrepresentation are foisted on families who have been admitted

to public housing bcause they are "good rent risks," that
is, because they have a stable (if low) and steady (if in-
sufficient) income. Some could, in fact, qualify for credit
in reputable downtown department stores, but, as in the
case of shopping for food, are reluctant to leave the neighborhood, feeling that their business is unwelcome in the
"white" stores, and fearing rejection, because they are
Negroes, if they apply for credit.

Negroes have too much and too long been not only the
victims of such charlatan businessmen, but also have
suffered exclusion both from employment in and ownership of business enterprises even within the ghetto. This
is the situation which gives rise to efforts to boycott liquor
stores, furniture stores, and other businesses in Harlem itself, and to campaigns to "buy black."

During the demonstrations of the summer of 1963 in
one section of the city protesting discriminatory hiring
practices of a certain restaurant chain, in which scores of
arrests were made, it turned out that the strongest opposition to the demonstrations within the business community
of that section was the crime syndicate. The businessmen
of organized crime were distressed by the demonstrations
because they caused a substantial increase in the numbers
of policemen assigned to the area and thus made it more
dangerous and difficult for drugs to be peddled and for
the numbers racket to operate. It is also likely that the
syndicate fears integration in business because it might
eventually require admitting Negroes to the rackets as well
as to legitimate businesses. The sanction invoked by the
syndicate to line up the opposition of businessmen and
others in the area was to threaten to call in and collect
loans made by the syndicate to otherwise legitimate businessmen who might be ready to go along with integration
in public accommodations, stores, and the like.

Or take hospitals. Not long ago I had a Negro client
who had taken her child one Sunday to a public play-

ground. The child, who was five years old, fell at the playground, hitting his head on the concrete surface. A few blocks away there is a private hospital, related, by the way, to one of the churches. The mother took her child there, and after waiting nearly an hour in the so-called emergency reception section, was finally interviewed by a doctor who explained that the mother would have to take the child to a public hospital, since she could not afford care at this institution and since that's what the public hospitals are for. Actually, of course, the private hospital could have been reimbursed by public welfare for any care given to the child, although at rates set by the welfare authorities rather than by the hospital administration. The nearest public hospital was four miles away, so, after having been turned away, the mother took the child there, walking part of the way, and going by bus part of the way, since she had no money for a taxi. After a further wait at the public hospital, the child was examined and it was found that he had suffered a serious injury which might permanently disable him. The doctors say that if the child had received prompt attention, the consequences of the injury would likely have been much less serious.

The mother in the case worked as a domestic. She told her employer about the matter, and he in turn reported it to me. It seemed likely that the reason the child had not been admitted to the private hospital was either because the family was poor or Negro, or, most likely, both. The mother, however, refused to make any formal complaint against the doctor and private hospital because, as she explained, she had no hope whatever that she could prevail. After all, why should she, a Negro, expect to be treated fairly or humanely by the law, any more than she had been by the private hospital, and, besides, the prosecution of the complaint would not heal her child. While the matter was being discussed, I called a friend of mine who is a reporter on one of the major New York newspapers, one which professes a great concern for human rights. I told him what had happened and suggested that it might be worth while publicizing this incident to call attention to discrimination in the private hospitals of the city. But he said that the incident was not newsworthy and that his paper received as many as a dozen reports a day of similar cases. "It's only a story for us," he said, "if the kid dies or if the injury is really grotesque!"

One of the uglier incidents, which *was* thought to be newsworthy, happened a few years ago in Harlem. A baby —just over two years old—developed a high fever, and his mother, a Negro, took him to a public hospital. The interne who examined the child told the mother that it was a minor respiratory infection, and prescribed some medicine. The mother took the child home, administered the medicine, but found in the next day or two that the fever did not abate. They returned to the hospital. This time a different interne was on duty, and he sent the mother and baby to the tuberculosis ward, saying that he suspected that this was the ailment. Testing there indicated that it was not, and again the mother and baby were discharged, after having been given some additional medicine. Three days later, when the baby's fever and discomfort persisted, the mother for the third time went to the hospital, waited her turn and, while the child was being examined by the doctor, it died. An autopsy subsequently established that the child had died, not from a respiratory infection, not from incipient tuberculosis, but from an infection caused by the bite of a rat. That's the sort of story that makes the newspapers. And that is the sort of incident—along with the playground case—that causes many Negroes to conclude that they can expect little care from hospitals or at least little competent care.

In short, in virtually every sector of the city's life— housing, education, and medical care, in business, politics, and employment, in the welfare administration and the

enforcement of the law—Negroes still suffer discrimination
and segregation, despite the legislative disclaimers of discrimination and the public promises of the politicians.

The tragedy and irony of Harlem is that while Negroes
have been lost in fondness for the image of Harlem as
the pioneer for all Negroes, Harlem has remained the
place and symbol of persistent, if sometimes subtle, discrimination: excluded from the housing, politics, lawful
protection, commercial enterprise, common culture, education, economic opportunity, sanitation, and free access
characteristic of the rest of the city and taken for granted
by the white people downtown.

The great affront to Harlem's pioneer destiny is that
Harlem still exists.

The Passion for Revenge

This is no report, by the way, about the extreme racists
within the Negro community, about the Black Muslims
or the Black Nationalists, although both exist and increasingly thrive in Harlem and in the other great urban ghettos
of the North, and they are by no means to be discounted
or underestimated.

Indeed, as far as the Muslims are concerned, they are
well financed—some say with funds from Arab sources—
and apparently they are congenial with the white racists
of the American Nazi Party; at least I myself have seen
some proof of their association with the American Nazis.
But these extremists—the Muslims—seem to have made a
fatal tactical mistake in their attempts to exploit the un-
rest and frustration and sentiment for revenge among
American Negroes, especially in the North. They have
required their adherents, not just to hate white men,
though that is their central doctrine and essential appeal;
they also require that their members renounce their re-

ligious inheritance—which in Harlem is either the Gospel tradition in Protestantism or, in the case of West Indian immigrants, Roman Catholicism—and embrace the indoctrination of a new and strange and unfamiliar religion (which, incidentally, bears little truthful resemblance to historic Islam), and to further submit to the discipline and rigorous piety of the new faith with respect to practical behavior from day to day. The Muslims have made hate too complicated and difficult and much too contingent upon a peculiar moralism to become a movement that receives mass support. Or so it seems to me, simply as an observer. Yet there is no doubt that the central emphasis of the extremists—like the Muslims—in the Negro communities of the North upon the simple hatred and rejection of white men because they are white men has enormous and increasing appeal among the Negroes of the city ghettos.

The great danger, for both Negroes and whites, is that some leader will emerge who will turn to his people and preach a blunt doctrine of hate and revenge. Because the ground has been so well prepared by extremists of both races, it will not be difficult to organize long-suppressed emotion and legitimate grievances into a powerful movement. If that comes to pass, the peaceful demonstrations in the streets will cease and peaceful protest will turn into chaos.

If that does happen, if there is a violent and bloody calamity, perhaps white Americans will then finally recognize, both in the North and the South, their profound indebtedness to the incumbent non-violent leadership of the Negro revolt for their great dignity and discipline and restraint.

Each day of die-hard indifference of white people in the North, each day of die-hard segregation in the South, invites disaster by making it more difficult for the Negro leadership favoring and practicing nonviolent protest to maintain its leadership. The nonviolent demonstrations have, after all, been going on for about five years on a significant scale, and reached a climax in the March on Washington in August of 1963. If from these demonstrations there is not some tangible result to which the present Negro leadership can point, it may be expected with certainty that the patience of Negroes will be exhausted and they will turn to other leaders and to other tactics, and turn from seeking redress of their grievances to taking revenge for the indignities they have suffered through three hundred years of slavery and segregation.

No account is given here of the extremists in Harlem, but the danger is that Harlem—along with each of the little Harlems of the nation—is driven to extremity.

One sign of how much racism tempts Negroes is the degree to which some leaders among them, who are not Muslims or Nationalists, feel constrained to imitate and recite racist doctrines. Some of the statements of Congressman Adam Clayton Powell reflect this change in the mood and militancy of Harlem. I recall, for another instance, attending a rally in Harlem some time ago, protesting police brutality. One of the speakers was a certain Negro minister whom I know well and who has been very moderate. It happens that this man is of very fair complexion and could easily "pass" for a white man. When he began his speech he apologized for his light color, whereupon he was booed by the crowd. He persisted in his apology and said that though he was light he knew the full burden of being a Negro in America. More booing. He changed his tactic and launched into the most provocative and virulent racist speech I think I have ever heard, advocating, among other things, black supremacy and resort to violence to oppose the violence of the police. This time the crowd was with him. He had sensed the depth of their hostility and had appeased it.

But there is a sequel to the incident. After the rally I

went to Greenwich Village where I had a date to have a drink with a white student who had just returned to the city from a Freedom Ride in Mississippi. As we sat in the restaurant, who should come in but the minister who had given the racist address at the rally. And guess who was with him? A white girl.

The important thing, so far as I am concerned, is not the duplicity of the minister—that is a problem he must live with all alone—but, rather, that he had felt that black supremacy and revenge had become so much the spirit of Harlem that he had to identify with it. He tried, first of all, to do that in his pitiful apology for his light skin, and, when that failed, he succeeded in gaining the crowd by outdoing even the professional racists in Harlem.

A particularly ominous sign of the extremities of Negro animosity is the emergence in the open of Negro anti-Semitism. It is a complex phenomenon, and one which has, as far as I can observe, been spawned over a very long time. Part of the picture is a sense of the uniqueness of the Negro cause as such, and a reluctance among Negroes to identify their cause with that of other minorities, not only the Jews, but also, for example, Puerto Ricans. This sentiment much prevails, in spite of the historic interest of the Jews in America in the civil rights of all citizens; and, in the case of the Puerto Ricans, in spite of their common problems. Negroes do not want to be lumped together with other minorities, but there is evidence of particular resentment at being associated with the Jews.

One reason for this is the direct competition now between Negroes and Jews in politics. In New York, in the succession of migrations and immigrations of the different ethnic groups, there has been a succession to political power that roughly parallels the order of the immigrations. For a while the Germans were politically powerful, but they were displaced by the Irish, and the Irish in time, by the Italians as the dominant group. But in this succession, the Jews did not receive their turn. They were not welcome in politics, although their numbers justified political recognition. It is only comparatively recently, through the device of a third party with preponderantly Jewish leadership and membership and through the so-called reform movement in the Democratic Party, that the Jews have received something like the political recognition and patronage status that their numbers and social and economic influence would have brought to other groups long since. The problem is that the Jews have belatedly emerged in great strength in city politics at just the time when the Negro demand for political power and patronage has become insistent. Consequently, the two minorities which have suffered the most harsh discrimination in city politics are now in the position of competing with each other for political power and patronage rather than being united in a common political cause.

But politics is not the only cause of Negro anti-Semitism. There are unfortunate instances in which Negroes have endured ill-treatment at the hands of individual Jews. A typical instance is when tenants live in slums where the landlord happens to be Jewish. I have had two cases where the landlords of abominable slums were rabbis—which hardly improves the image of the Jews in the eyes of Negroes. The fact is, too, that some of the furniture dealers who have victimized Negroes moving into new housing have been Jewish, and this further feeds anti-Semitism.

Even the substantial philanthropy of Jews for the civil rights struggle and their sincere sympathy for the plight of the Negroes are greeted with suspicion and resentment. "Who are they to speak for us?" is a common form which this hostility takes. "Nobody but a Negro can know what it means to be a Negro" is the sentiment which rejects identification on the part of Jews with the Negro cause.

Yet the overriding reason for Negro anti-Semitism, as

far as I can discern, is that it is some awful emulation of the anti-Semitism so long prevalent and so unyielding among middle- and upper-class white Protestants and Catholics. For generations, these citizens, who have been ascendant in American society, have made anti-Semitism a mark of social and political status, something which, while it seldom took the form of open persecution, was, and still too much remains, an accepted attitude and practice.

Insofar as this is the basis of Negro anti-Semitism, it places white Christians in an excruciating position. On one hand, they must now stand beside the Jews and share with the Jews the hostility of Negroes toward all white people; but, at the same time, they themselves are authors of one form of that very hostility—the anti-Semitism of Negroes which imitates the anti-Semitism of white Protestants and Catholics. Such is the economy of judgment.

In any event, now it is at least in the open, no longer latent and snide and festering, but brought into the open by the boycotts of Jewish merchants in Harlem, the rent strikes against some Jewish landlords, and the attempts to integrate some unions and industries that have heretofore been predominantly white and Jewish. Now that it is in the open, perhaps it can and will be dealt with in a way which both affirms the uniqueness of the Negro and the grandeur of the Negro's struggle, and also in some way works a reconciliation among Negroes and Jews and white Christians.

The spirit of revenge which stalks the streets of Harlem and the other urban ghettos is one which increasingly regards any association in public between Negro and white as suspect as a guilty association, one which calls into question the loyalty and racial pride of the Negro, one in which the Negro is thought to be tempted or intimidated or cajoled or purchased into some compromise of his integrity and identity as a Negro.

An event like the censure of A. Philip Randolph, the distinguished leader of the American Negro Labor Council, and virtually the patriarch of Harlem, by the Executive Council of the AFL–CIO for his exposure of racial discrimination in the unions—the proof of which has been amply documented—abets the suspicion that when a Negro tries to negotiate or collaborate with whites—even those who protest most that they are liberals—he must either betray himself and his people or suffer humiliation.

Even the word "Negro" is dropping from usage, in favor of the term "black man," in order to express the pride a man who is black should have in being black, and the disdain that black men should have toward white men.

There was a time, for example, when prostitution in New York involved supplying Negro girls to white patrons from downtown, and when some brothels in Harlem catered largely to white customers. Those days are gone. A Negro prostitute does not have white customers any more, no matter what the price, because to associate with white people is a disloyalty to her race and people and their cause, just as much for a prostitute as for any Uncle Tom in politics or the churches.

The intensity of the rejection of association with white people apparent among Negroes should be enough to put to rest the red herring in the civil rights crisis regarding intermarriage. The fact is, bluntly, that most Negroes hate white people. When there is, as there will surely be, integration in public life in America—housing and education and politics and jobs and public accommodations—there will not suddenly be a great increase in marriages between the races. At least I have detected no greater interest in the subject among Negroes than among whites. And why should there be much interest in the subject? Nobody is interested in marriage in the abstract. Marriage is a personal issue and decision, and it remains that with respect to marriages between the races, if marriage in a serious

and responsible sense is being contemplated. The intermarriage issue is empirically baseless and, where ad-
vanced as an obstacle to the right of Negroes to be received
and welcomed as citizens in public life, represents a gross,
irrational, and stupid vanity on the part of white people.

And it is, aptly, the subject of ridicule.

I know a seminary professor, a native white Southerner,
who is a strong advocate of the Negro cause. Long before
the present crisis, he was an eloquent and effective witness in the South for civil rights. He has a very attractive
daughter, eligible for marriage. He tells me that he is invariably asked, after giving a speech in support of civil
rights, what he himself would do if a Negro proposed to
his daughter. His stock answer to this query is to say:
"First of all I would ask him whether he is a Protestant, a
Catholic, or a Jew!"

Or, to show how ridiculous this intermarriage issue is
from another point of view, I recollect recently being in
the South and meeting an elderly Negro gentleman. He, as
it happens—and as is the case with many Negroes of slave
ancestry in this country—had a white father. Asked one
day by a white Southerner about this, he replied that he
indeed had a white father. The conversation was overheard
by another Negro, who, after the white Southerner had
departed, approached my friend and said: "Tom, don't
you ever, ever do that again. Don't you ever admit to a
white Southerner that your father was a white man—you
tell 'em that it was your mother who was white!"

In other words, intermarriage, when posed as an abstract and impersonal issue, is irrelevant to the civil rights
of Negro citizens. There is no serious evidence of any
significant interest, abstractly and impersonally, in intermarriage among either whites or Negroes, whereas there
is plenty of evidence of the slavery era having fostered
many, many interracial liaisons, and, later on, evidence of
Negro prostitution for white customers. So let the specter

of intermarriage be put to rest. The issue it really raises is the sexual ethics of white men outside of marriage, both in the days of slavery and in the days of the traveling salesman. And let two people fall in love and marry if they are given the gift of love, even though they be of different races, though they be different in any other way. They will have, and probably will continue to have for a long time, more difficulties than most marriages in this society. But the issue, then, is not so much society's as theirs, and if under the burdens which this society adds to any interracial marriage, they survive and prosper as man and wife and as a family, that only enhances the dignity and maturity of their love. It is, in any case, no reason to oppose or deny any Negro his place and his prerogatives as an American citizen.

Ironically, though the passion for revenge is active and, I fear, increasing within the Negro community, especially in the urban North, that which has subdued and controlled this passion is the same thing which, in the end, may be the proximate cause of vengeance and violence. What has mainly quieted the advocates of violence and counseled extraordinary restraint in the Negro revolution has been the leadership crisis within the Negro community itself. If any proof were needed—which none is—of the profound humanity of Negroes, it is supplied by the infighting and pettiness and personality conflicts, the competitiveness and throat-cutting within the Negro "establishment" itself. They are just like white people: scrapping and fighting and destroying each other. In all this maneuvering and internal struggle for leadership of the Negro revolution, the rest of the nation has gained some time to acknowledge and respond to the revolution. But now that time is running out, and if the Negro leadership crisis (among CORE, NAACP, SCLC, the Urban League, the student movements, the black racists, and the remaining Uncle Toms) is not resolved, then racial chaos is surely in store for America. The masses of Negro people have, at last, been moved. They will not wait long for a leader, nor dally about who the leader is; they will move by themselves, if need be, without a leader, and the revolution will become an insurrection. They are tired, they are frustrated, they are angry, they are impatient, they are aggressive, they are ready for a leader, but—as the summer riots evidence—they are also ready to go into the streets without a leader, all by themselves, as other men have had to do from time to time to defend and vindicate their own humanity.

The Depths of Estrangement

If one looks today at the cities of the North, where the decisive struggle in the Negro revolution is taking shape, the conclusion is inescapable that the estrangement between the races in the North is virtually complete. Despite the Northern civil rights legislation, despite the commissions on human rights, despite the ceremonial presence of Negroes in public life, despite the liberalism of many white Northerners, despite good intentions and naïve sincerity, racism has not been exorcised; indeed, racism increases. It not only becomes more evident and intransigent among white people, as Negroes press their claims with greater vigor and determination, but, latent in Negroes, it begins to emerge and flourish among them.

The truth is that in the years since the beginning of substantial migration of Negroes from the South to the Northern cities, and of the immigration of Negroes from the West Indies to the Northern cities, there has been precious little honest, honorable, or significant communication between the races. The platitudes of tolerance, it turns out, conceal the practice of discrimination, for the American idea of tolerance—though it be less vehement than South Africa's apartheid—is, after all, a generically similar doctrine of racial coexistence. The promises of acceptance, freedom, and society in the Northern city have not been validated in education, jobs, housing, politics, or the equal protection of the law. Everything seemed fine for many years, but the condition of that tranquillity was the acquiescence of Negro citizens in a second-class status and a ghetto existence, separated from the comforts, mobility, and opportunities of life in the outer city.

The platitudes and promises, the liberalism and benign intentions of Northern white society during the last fifty years in which the Negro migration to the cities has taken place, mean little when it remains true to this day that eighty-five per cent of all Negroes in metropolitan New York, for example, live in one or another of five neighborhoods which are virtually entirely black, and, in consequence, send their children to black schools, worship in black churches, dine at black restaurants, attend black movie theaters, and, in all the ordinary facets of community life, associate almost entirely with their fellow Negroes. The main contact with the white people for the multitude of Northern Negroes has been when some Negro has left Harlem to go to work—as a domestic in an East Side penthouse, as a Sanitation Department employee to collect the waste of the rest of the city, or to wait on tables in a downtown restaurant which seldom has a Negro customer, to scrub the floors of empty offices late at night, to sell body and dignity to a white businessman for a night, or to entertain white people in a club or bar.

Of course, in all this time, some Negroes have made the grade and have achieved a certain acceptance in, and access to, white society. Some have made it, as has been earlier mentioned, by becoming quislings. Only a few have made it without that humiliation. One is Dr. Anna Arnold Hedgeman. Despite the eminence she has achieved, it is constructive to see how she constantly had to resist being "used" by white society.

Dr. Hedgeman began her professional career as a school teacher in the dark regions of Mississippi, but later, after some years of community work in the Midwest, moved to New York, where she was an executive with the Harlem Y.W.C.A., engaged in a multitude of efforts to raise the educational, occupational, and cultural level of Harlem. Long before the present sit-ins and demonstrations —indeed before some of the leaders of the present Negro revolution were born—she and others, including A. Philip Randolph, were engaged in trying to qualify Negroes for jobs in urban society and then in trying to secure jobs for them. The reason the major department stores in New York have Negro salespeople today is a credit to Anna Hedgeman's pioneering work twenty years ago. From her baptism in teaching and community work, she went to Washington as the Executive Director of the National Council for a Permanent Fair Employment Practices Committee. She led the effort to enact legislation to make the wartime FEPC permanent. President Truman's support of this legislation motivated Mrs. Hedgeman to campaign and to raise funds from Negroes across the country for Truman's re-election in 1948. As a result she was appointed Assistant to Oscar Ewing, the head of the Federal Security Agency.

Mrs. Hedgeman later returned to New York City, was an assistant manager in the first campaign of Robert Wagner for Mayor of New York, and after his election, was invited to join his administration. It soon developed that this was an invitation to become an Uncle Tom. It was an invitation to have a Negro presence adorn the city administration but not engage in any serious work or exercise any significant influence on the policies of the administration.

Three different jobs were offered to Mrs. Hedgeman.

One was a post already held by a Negro. She refused this on the grounds that it represented no gain for her people or recognition for her if she simply replaced another Negro in a position that had already been allocated to Negroes, in accordance with the *de facto* ethnic quota system which prevails in so much of New York politics.

Then she was asked if she would become a seventh deputy police commissioner, again replacing a Negro. Mrs. Hedgeman had no specific qualifications for such a position and would have been consigned there to a merely ceremonial role. She would have no part of that, in spite of the salary, prestige, and publicity to be gained by accepting.

Finally, she was tendered an office in the Mayor's Cabinet, which she did accept. In the Mayor's Cabinet in New York, there are several positions of ministers without portfolio, often acting as trouble shooters in city affairs, reporting and directly responsible to the Mayor without going through departmental channels. In practice, these offices are dispensed in a way that insures the ethnic balance the Mayor's administration needs to attract and hold support from the various ethnic blocs in the city's voting population. In appointing Mrs. Hedgeman, Mayor Wagner may have felt especially inspired, for here he had a representative of three of the city's neglected minorities: Mrs. Hedgeman was not only a Negro, but a woman and a Protestant!

The day of the inauguration came and, with suitable fanfare, the Cabinet was sworn in. It was not long before Mrs. Hedgeman discovered that she was not expected to show up at City Hall or to maintain an office there. Her function was to decorate occasions when it seemed important for the image of the administration to have a Negro or a woman or a Protestant, or some combination thereof, on the scene. Even after being sworn in as Assistant to the Mayor, she was again unsuccessfully offered

the police assignment—an inept attempt to relegate her to
a nominal and vassal role. There was some consternation
at City Hall in the days and weeks that followed, because
of Mrs. Hedgeman's insistence that she wanted to be a
functioning, working member of the administration, not a
ceremonial, occasional officer. It became clear that she
was not interested in patronage for herself, but in accom-
plishing something for her people.

Eventually, as might have been predicted, Anna Hedgeman resigned from the Wagner administration. Her life
of authentic concern shows her to have been a pioneer
in the present civil rights demonstrations which have now
forever established that Negroes will no longer be appeased by promises, platitudes, and nominal recognition.

It was Anna Hedgeman who, years ago had foreseen,
before almost anyone else, either black or white, the
gravity of the estrangement between Negroes and whites
in American society, especially in the urban North. One
afternoon she said to me: "Very few Negroes and white
people are in real communication with each other. Those
of us who can and do speak honestly, as you and I do,
must keep in touch and help others to learn the quality of
communication necessary if the races are to be reconciled.
This will be very hard and will become more difficult as
the crisis deepens, but that just makes it all the more important that we keep in touch."

I remember, not long ago, spending hours on the tele-
phone receiving calls, in turn, from some of the Negro
leaders in the civil rights struggle, and then from some of
the white church leaders who had, somewhat belatedly and
somewhat suddenly, become committed to direct action
in the struggle. The calls were distressing because they
showed how radical the estrangement of the races is, even
(perchance especially) in the churches. There were two
sorts of calls, on the occasion that I recollect: One kind
came from white ecclesiastical officers who reported that

the churches had decided to enter into direct action in support of the civil rights of Negroes, but they wanted to know whether this or that Negro was the one with whom to discuss the matter. The other kind of call came from Negroes who, having received inquiries from the white ecclesiastics, wanted to know if they should bother to meet with them, because they were not really sure that those who had called them could be trusted, and they wanted to know if I trusted the white people who had been involved in such overtures. This is not only proof of how wide the alienation between the races has become— it is not even widely known whom to begin to try to talk with—but it is also evidence of how fragile and inadequate the avenues of tolerance and humanism are for serious and candid communication between the races.

I remember, also (this is another type of example), being invited more than two years ago to lecture at Columbia Law School on the racial crisis in the city, especially as it pertained to politics. I spoke before an audience of bright, young, white law students. They listened to the lecture, I thought, in a rather sullen way. The burden of the lecture is the burden of this chapter of my book—that one who becomes somehow immersed in some of the visceral and brutal realities of the racial crisis cannot escape a premonition of chaos and imminent disaster.

What I had to report that night was later to become the substance of an article, "Race, Religion and Revenge," published by *The Christian Century* in their issue of February 14, 1962. I gave the speech and said, I trust, what, as nearly as I could figure out as a white man, was and is the truth about the relations between races in the Northern cities. When I finished, there were a lot of comments from the law students. They fell, roughly, into two categories. The first alleged that I had been too harsh and "pessimistic" about the relations between the races in America, and these assertions were documented by the

experiences of some of the students themselves, such as
the fact that several of them had been exposed to Negroes
in New York—taxi drivers and waiters and the like—and
had been treated by them, in these situations, with civility
and courtesy. After further discussion, it soon became
apparent to the students that the casual contacts they had
experienced with taxi drivers, elevator operators, waiters,
and so on, did not constitute significant, nor even honest
and honorable, communication with Negroes in the city.
So that line of attack on my paper was abandoned. The
line which took its place was much more revealing. They
said, in effect, "Well, the trouble with you, Stringfellow, is
that you have lived so long among *them* that you have
begun to think like *they* do!" Their objection, finally, as
far as I could comprehend it, was that I, by living and
working those years in Harlem, had somehow ceased to
be a white man, or at least had lost the capacity and
authority to speak as a white man—through, I suppose,
overexposure to Negroes.

If that be the case, let it be.

All this time I had thought that there is something
unique about being a human being, something which tran-
scends all of our human differences and diversities,
whether of race or age or class or profession or sex or
wealth or whatever. And if it must come to pass, in the
agonizing tensions and fears which characterize the racial
crisis, that any white man regards me—or any one of a
number of other white men—as traitors to our race and
heritage, *then let that be*. It can only prove how deep and
pathetic the estrangement of the races has become in this
society, so fond of boasting of its democracy and regard
for humanity.

The estrangement *is* almost complete. The proof of that
is in the so-called white liberals of the North, as much as,
or perhaps more than, in the white segregationists of the
South. For these white Northerners, in their professions of

liberalism toward the Negroes, suffer from a mentality which still assumes that white men retain the initiative in the racial crisis and that white men have, and should continue to have, the prerogative of determining the pace of the Negro's emancipation and the terms of his reception into full citizenship. "What do the Negroes want?" they ask, not discerning that this very question embodies the essence of white supremacy, even though perhaps it be a more subtle and more genteel white supremacy than that characteristic of the irrational and crude segregationists of the Deep South.

That question—"What do the Negroes want?"—presupposes that what the Negroes want is for the whites to give, as if, in this society, the whites retain some right to dispense to the Negroes or to anybody else what is theirs by birthright and citizenship and, in truth, by their common humanity. White men have no authority—legally or morally—to rule upon any demands of Negroes. White men have only to acknowledge and honor at last the same civil and human rights for Negroes that they treasure for themselves.

Yet the condescension among Northern whites is still conspicuous and, one might add, obnoxious. It is, in its own fashion, much more embittering and provocative, much more incitive and die-hard than the rabid, traditional, and sometimes pathological racism of the South. It not only assumes that whites hold the initiative in the resolution of the racial crisis, which is a fantasy, since the initiative has now conclusively passed into the hands of the Negroes, as the past few years attest; but it also still treats participation by white citizens in the civil rights struggle as a "good cause"—as a cause that ought to be supported by people of principle and conscience, just as aid to refugees might also be supported with time and money, or just as the work of the United Nations might be upheld with words and occasional actions.

The only thing is that this is no "good cause." Not at least in the sense that refugee assistance or apologetics for the United Nations may be. The Negro revolution is no ordinary charity to which enlightened whites should give their donations and their names. The Negro revolution is, rather, an authentic *revolution,* in which the whole prevailing social order of the nation is being overturned in the face of three hundred years of slavery, segregation, discrimination, and *de facto* racism throughout the country. Every important institution in the public life of the nation—education, employment, unions, churches, entertainment, housing, politics, commerce, investment, welfare, transportation, public accommodations—is immediately affected by this revolution, and this revolution will not spend its course until every such institution surrenders to its objectives. The only real question is the means by which the inevitable integration of American public life will take place—peaceably or violently, realistically or obstinately, today or tomorrow.

This is no "good cause," in the conventional sense of the term. And to treat it as such—as so many Northern liberals still do—is in itself condescending and stupid. How, then, should white people, especially those in the North, treat this issue?

First of all, they must surrender their prerogative of decision. *First of all,* they must face the fact that the real decisions determining how the racial crisis will be resolved are for the Negroes to make. *First of all,* they must give up the idea that they have and should continue indefinitely to have the prerogatives of white supremacy. *First,* white people must die to that mentality by suffering the hostility and rejection of Negroes and by risking their lives and the future of this society in the hands of the Negroes.

That is the preface to reconciliation between black men and white men.

Chapter Five
EPIPHANY

I stopped by a bar in the neighborhood to have a beer.

It's a cruddy place—dimly lit and dirty and drafty—but not a dismal place. A lot of people live there—it is a sort of parlor for those who have none in their tenements: people sit around, talk and laugh, argue and drink, listen or dance to the noise from the jukebox.

I sat on a stool and the bartender brought me a beer. He mumbled a greeting and made an obscene complaint about how hot the day had been. I agreed with him.

Then Teddy came in. He had had to spend a little time in jail. I had heard that he was out and had hoped he might turn up. He is a Negro, maybe twenty-one, a school drop-out. We shook hands and he sat down on the next stool. He did the talking. He was mad and bitter. He'd been back more than a week and had looked for a job, but had everywhere been turned down.

"There just ain't no jobs for me, man," he said, "there just ain't no jobs for Negroes in this town."

He had been this route before. Since school he had had a few menial jobs here and there and off and on, but nothing regular and nothing going anywhere. That's partly how he got into trouble—he had no job, needed money, and got caught trying to get some. Now there still were no jobs for him, especially with a record.

"Why was I born black?" He blamed his mother.

"White men are all sons-of-bitches." He decided to blame white mothers instead.

I listened to his long, passionate, hostile, frustrated speech.

"One thing, Bill," he announced finally, "you've always been my friend." I laughed, and he remembered that I am a white man.

He laughed, too, and then we had another beer to celebrate.

If Negroes become disillusioned, if they now grow impatient and restive and aggressive, if they begin to regard the promises of human recognition and acceptance in the urban North as shopworn and less attractive than rejection of white people and white society, if they resent the intransigence of segregation in the South, then they are radically disenchanted with the churches.

And who is to undo their disenchantment? What is to refute their image of the churches as imperious, condescending, unknowing, indifferent, unloving, hypocritical? Oh, one *can* name some few congregations here and there in both the North and the South where such an image is unfair and untrue, but that is, in part, the point: these are so few that they are exceptional and conspicuous. One can name some white Christians, too, particularly some white clergy, who have risked their lives and their status in white society by their own involvement in the racial crisis, but these are few compared to the pathetic majority of white Christians in the land.

The issue now is whether the witness of these exceptional congregations and of these few white Christians will not be blotted from the consciousness of the Negroes by the massive impression of the churches as lily-white institutions and of white Christians as white supremacists and by the relentless pressures upon Negroes to disassociate themselves from white institutions and white people for the sake of a more militant Negro solidarity.

The Cynicism of the Churches

The churches of white society in America have largely
forfeited any claim to leadership in the relations between
the races, and, to a great extent, have not even seriously
understood those relations in terms of the Christian faith;
their active concern in the last century has been, to an
overwhelming degree, limited to the nominal pronouncements of church assemblies and ecclesiastical authorities.
But few of these pronouncements have betrayed a theological understanding of the relations of the races. Mainly,
they have repeated the empty dogmas of humanism and
the platitudes of tolerance.

And, often, the whole subject has simply been ignored
altogether. As true a symbol of the diffidence and nominal
concern of the churches regarding race as I know of, is
seen in an incident that took place nearly a hundred years
ago in the House of Bishops of the Protestant Episcopal
Church. The Episcopal Church takes some pride in the
fact that it was not separated geographically during the
Civil War, as so many of the other churches of Protestantism were. But that does not mean that there were no
strong feelings among Episcopalians, North and South,
during and after the Civil War. During a session of the
House of Bishops as the war ended and the Reconstruction crisis began, there was a vehement controversy as to
whether the pastoral letter to be issued by the Bishops to
the people of the church should deal directly with the
issues of the war and the Reconstruction. So heated was
the debate that some Bishops moved that no letter at all
be issued, lest it divide the church. Others wanted the
letter to take up the problems at that time thrust upon
the church by the emergence of Biblical criticism. A letter
was drafted which dealt both with the issues confronting

the nation in the Reconstruction and those raised for the church by Biblical criticism; but the letter as finally adopted and approved dealt only with "so much as relates to rationalism." On the Reconstruction crisis, the Bishops were silent.

Things have not changed much since then. In the early days of the present racial crisis, the churches were most hesitant to take any position on the sit-in demonstrations until long after many secular institutions had given their support. The party platform pronouncements of both the Democratic and Republican conventions of 1960 on the sit-ins, for example, were far more definite than the statements at the same time by the assemblies of the major denominations who made statements (and most did not). The churches, insofar as they have addressed the racial issue in this society, have either been silent or timid; where there have been any pronouncements, they have typically followed changes in the public consensus and in the status quo.

That was evident as recently as January, 1963, during the National Conference on Religion and Race, held in Chicago under the auspices of the National Catholic Welfare Conference, the National Council of Churches, and the Synagogue Council of America. The Conference was so out of touch with the realities of the racial revolt in America that, in the main, it failed to recognize or address them. What went unnoticed at the Conference was that even as it met, pickets and demonstrators were ready to march in the streets. What went ignored in the Conference were such issues of religion and race as the Black Muslims and Negro anti-Semitism. The Conference was spared hearing such harsh realities of the racial crisis as these.

Another indication of the massive indifference to and ignorance of the intensity, pathology, and alienation represented by the racial crisis was the manner in which Ne-

groes were treated in the Conference leadership itself.
Apart from the single exception of Martin Luther King,
no Negro spokesman was on the program of the Conference, except for those who introduced other speakers,
entertained the delegates, or prayed over the deliberations.
Uncle Tom was the most popular Negro at the National
Conference on Religion and Race. His days are gone forever, engulfed in the tides of the revolution the nation now
suffers. But it is important to remember that one of his
last days was spent at this Conference of the churches
of the land, saying "yes, suh" to the most banal clichés
within the vocabulary of white religionists, praising the
"progress" that has been achieved in race relations in
America within the very shadow of Chicago's teeming
black ghettos, and reciting in unison the sentimental
psalms of interfaith meetings about the fatherhood of God
and the brotherhood of men.

I raise no particular question about the nice intentions,
good will, or benign disposition of anybody at the Conference, but I do say that the churches have to be realistic
and face and state the truth about the American racial
crisis; they must speak and act out of the depths of faith
and not merely as those who follow the status quo, whatever it happens to be, and not as those fearful of risking
their reputations and possessions if they speak propheti-
cally in faith.

The truth is that this Conference was too little, too late,
and too lily-white. The truth is that it represented a mentality which continues to assume that significant initiative
in the racial crisis remains with the churches of the nation, while, in fact, the churches more often than not have
absented themselves from the scenes of racial crises, both
in the South and in the North.

The events in the streets have long since outdistanced
the National Conference on Religion and Race and that
which it symbolizes: the reluctance of the churches to be

involved in the racial crisis beyond the point of pontifi-
cation. What has happened in the months since the Conference, both in the North and the South, both inside and
outside the churches, shows how woefully the churches
have underestimated and misunderstood the gravity and
vehemence and passion of the racial crisis in America.

In that time, dogs have been set upon citizens for complaining about the deprivation of their civil rights, hoses
have been turned upon Negroes who sought equal protection of the law, tear gas and electric cattle prods have
been used to disperse pickets, clubs have bashed in the
heads of demonstrators protesting discrimination in hiring, housing, and education; children have been arrested;
jails have been so overcrowded with those seeking redress
of their grievances that stables have had to be converted
into makeshift prisons. A church has been bombed, and
the first few of what will certainly be very many—if the
nation continues on this collision course—have died. The
revolution in race relations has exposed the witness of the
churches in these last years—nay, in these past hundred
years—as at least a little corny, if not, indeed, profane.

After all, it has not escaped the notice of Negroes that
for many Roman Catholics, parochial schools have in
fact been supported as a way of continuing to give their
children a segregated education; and that, for example,
among New York's nearly two thousand Protestant congregations, very few are more than nominally integrated.
Occasional Negro visitors are not, as yet, turned away
from Sunday services, but not many congregations welcome sincerely and, much less in the affection of Christ,
the Negro who wishes to become a communicant. And
where the clergy explain that housing segregation means
that there are no nearby Negroes to welcome into their
churches, how often have they or their lay people done
anything to oppose or threaten neighborhood segregation?
Remember the churches which have quit and closed down

when Negroes moved into a neighborhood and the whites moved out? Or recall the congregations who, to this day, refuse to integrate because that would divide the present membership of the church; yet they do not seem to care how radically the church is divided by segregation. What about the church-supported summer camps and schools and hospitals and homes for the aged, where the only Negroes on the premises are those employed to wash the dishes or operate the elevators or empty bedpans?

Where is the ecclesiastical authority so farsighted that he is today engaged in recruiting Negroes for the ordained ministry, and is prepared to support such candidates not only in seminary but through college, in order that an integrated church may be served by an integrated clergy? Most ecclesiastical authorities still persist in the practice of placing Negro clergy in Negro missions—timid, one suspects, of the uproar and, incidentally, of the economic difficulties that would surely accompany any other policy.

Meanwhile, the churches and other religious societies of American Negroes have begun to be censured and suspected and openly denounced as accomplices of discrimination and segregation. The people of these churches will no longer be appeased by gospels which locate God out of this world, nor by the disguise or minimizing of present sufferings in assurances of extravagant blessings on some later day.

Negroes are tragically tempted into apostasy, on one hand by the aloofness and intransigence of the churches of white society, and, on the other, by the frivolousness, vested interests, and irrelevance of many of the Negro churches and sects.

At both extremities of the spectrum of the Negro revolution, the churches are being rejected as having no viable word to say in the present crisis or, beyond that, of not having the courage or integrity to act. On one extreme are the Black Muslims who have made renunciation of the churches, as bulwarks of white supremacy, a central part of their appeal and platform. But at the other end, when the time came for the most moderate and nonviolent civil rights leadership in the South to give form and unity to the several factions in the movement, and to offer a symbol and an ideational basis, the image and ideology to which they turned was the person and philosophy of Gandhi, not the figure and faith of Christ. Somehow Gandhi appealed as a more universal symbol than Christ. And if this is so, it is on the heads of white Christians in America for smearing the image of Christ by making Him into a white Anglo-Saxon Protestant and for making their churches into shrines for the idolization of that image of Jesus. White Christians, perhaps especially the Protestants, bear the responsibility not only for the rejection of the churches by the Negroes, not only for the exclusion of Negroes from their congregations, but for the rejection, by both the Muslims and the Gandhians, of Christ Himself.

Let no white Christian boast, either, about the recent, belated entrance of some of the churches and some of the leaders of the churches into direct action in the racial crisis, notably in the participation of some fifty thousand white people, largely recruited through the churches, in the March on Washington in August, 1963. I welcome this sudden turnabout in the churches as much as any man, particularly because it seemed to me important that the Washington March itself be noticeably integrated. But those who marched that day from the white churches have no reason for pride. By the summer of 1963, the Negro revolt had gained such momentum that it had become as clear as anything ever does in this history that sooner or later, with violence or peacefully, the Negro revolution could not be turned back, and would prevail. Moreover, it has long since been irrevocably established, mainly by the decisions of the Supreme Court of the United States, that the public policy favored integration in all essential aspects of American public life—schools, housing, education and employment, transportation and public accommodations. The churches and the people of the churches who have now become committed to direct action in the racial crisis do so as recalcitrants upon whom it has finally dawned, despite a multitude of signs and warnings, that there is an authentic and momentous revolution going on and that its outcome is not in serious doubt; they now join the side which is winning. I myself have been told by one high-ranking ecclesiastic just that—and just that bluntly. Even in this burst of direct involvement in the demonstrations by some of the churches, they are again followers of public policy, neither leaders in social change nor prophets in the land. So let none boast.

Meanwhile, most white churches and their members are still uninvolved and uncommitted. Although they may not admit it to themselves, they remain obstinately opposed to the social changes, both in the churches and society, which are being brought about by the Negro revolution. The churches have, with few exceptions, refused to risk their wealth or use their enormous economic power in American society in the racial struggle, except as they continue to commit it intentionally, or by default, to segregation and discrimination. The churches of main-line, predominantly white American Protestantism have investments of staggering magnitude in business and industry, not only endowments controlled and invested by denominational mission boards, but also investments held by regional jurisdictions and by the larger parishes in the cities and the suburbs. How many of them have ever even examined their investment portfolios to find out whether the enterprises in which they have substantial holdings practice discrimination in hiring or job training? A few have, but most have not even considered such an involvement in the struggle; among those who have given this consideration, the view has usually been taken that it is inappropriate for the churches to use their economic power for social ends. They overlook the fact that their economic power *is* already committed to social ends wherever it is part of the investment in enterprises which practice segregation and discrimination. And they overlook the fact that the most effective weapon in the racial crisis has not been legislation, or even court decisions, or demonstrations, or federal troops, but economic sanctions. When the white merchants of Birmingham began to feel the economic pinch because of racial disturbances there, negotiations began between whites and Negroes; when industry began to desert Little Rock, after the school crisis there, Little Rock began to moderate segregation in public accommodations; when Negroes have rallied their own economic power and boycotted stores and industries in some of the Northern cities, jobs have been opened to them. When white Americans realize that the economic survival of the whole nation depends upon the gainful employment of the twenty million Negroes of America, and the education and opportunity prerequisite to such employment, they will suffer the loss of their obstinance to integration.

And it is just that which is now at stake—survival of the nation—in the Negro revolution, and no white man need become involved in the revolution, as has been said, because he thinks of it as a "good cause." He will become involved, he will support the revolution, because his own life and livelihood are just as much at issue as that of the Negro.

White Americans, perhaps especially those of the churches, have also to confront another reality of the racial crisis. Most white people, specifically the more benign, well-intentioned, "liberal" whites of the North, still vainly deceive themselves that the initiative in the racial crisis resides with the whites. But the initiative has al-

ready decisively passed from white to black, and white
people are no longer in a position of determining or
dominating what will happen next in the revolution, or
whether or not this revolt will turn increasingly to violence. White people are in a position of waiting to respond
to whatever initiatives come from the Negroes. While
waiting, they might well spend their time thanking God
that there has not yet emerged to lead the Negroes, either
in the North or the South, a militant, charismatic fanatic;
while waiting, they might also spend some time in giving thanks for Martin Luther King and his advocacy and
example of nonviolence, as the best friend white Americans have ever had—not excepting George Washington.

Christians among the white people in America will
have, as well, some other things to ponder. For their concern about the racial crisis and their involvement in it is
not limited to, or essentially expressed by, exorcism of
segregation, or, beyond that, the achievement of public
integration in American society generally and in the
churches in American society. Christians are in the first
instance concerned about how reconciliation between
black men and white men is to be attained. That goes
not only far beyond the interest or province of the civil
rights movement, or of the law of the land, or of the work
or witness of church assemblies. Christians know and confess reconciliation as a work and gift of God Himself.
Christians behold the reconciliation which God gives to
men in this world as His unique work in Christ, and they
know that the crucifixion is inherent in this reconciliation
which God works among men. The design, sequence,
structure, drama, and fulfillment of reconciliation focus
upon the crucifixion. There is no reason—least of all for
Christians—to expect that it will be otherwise in the reconciliation of the races now in such profound alienation
and conflict in this country.

The Way to Live

How then, in this time and in this crisis, is such reconciliation wrought? What signs are to be seen of the cruciform nature of reconciliation?

At the center of the drama of the Crucifixion of Christ is God, bearing the burden of the hostility of both Israel and Rome—in fact, of all men and nations—to Himself. That hostility is dissipated and absolved by His own assumption of the estrangement between God and men. The Church, called to be the Body of Christ in this world, and the people of the Church, called to be the members of His Body in this world, share in that self-same ministry and service in the world.

The central witness of the Church in the racial crisis is to bear the rejection of white people by Negroes, provoked by three centuries of exclusion and exploitation of Negroes by whites, and to bear this terrible, compounding hostility between the races without protest or complaint, without concern for innocence or guilt (that is for God's judgment and forgiveness to reveal), in other words, in the love of Christ for the whole world.

One witness of God's power in reconciling men is known now in the death of Lou Marsh.

Lou Marsh died in New York City at ten minutes after nine on the evening of January 9th, 1963.

At first his death was not much noticed, although it would have been, had not the metropolitan newspapers been struck at the time. Not that Marsh was famous in a way the world would necessarily remember him, but his death was one of the more shocking homicides in memory, even in New York City. If there had been newspapers, at least the tabloids, in their own way, would have celebrated Lou's death.

Lou worked for the New York City Youth Board, assigned to one of East Harlem's juvenile gangs—the self-styled Untouchables. I remember suggesting that he apply for such a job, and later wrote to the Youth Board authorities recommending him for it. When he decided to take the job, he called to tell me of what he hoped to accomplish.

Lou was beaten to death by four guys. He had somehow persuaded the gang—the Untouchables—not to go ahead with a rumble to which they had committed themselves against the Playboys, another gang in the neighborhood. Some of the older boys—alumni, so to speak, of one of the gangs in question—wanted the issue between the two gangs to be settled in the traditional way, according to the canons of gang society, by a rumble. They resented the fact that Lou mediated the dispute, or at least accomplished an armistice. Evidently they were humiliated that the younger boys in the gangs followed Lou's counsel rather than their own. So they ambushed Lou and beat him savagely. He lived for two days in the hospital, unconscious. Then he died. One doctor told me that the damage to his brain was so severe and gruesome that if, by some chance, he had survived, he would probably not have been able to function in any ordinary way as a human being. He most likely would have been grotesquely invalided, living on as a vegetable.

Lou died, it seems, an awful death, but a death that was apparently somehow better for him and for those who loved him than mere survival would have been.

Among those who knew of Lou's death, but did not know Lou, there were easy, stereotyped reactions. Mayor Wagner observed that this was the first time in fifteen years that a Youth Board worker had been slain in the line of duty, and said that he was outraged. I am afraid that Lou would have been more amused than anything else at the Mayor's vague promises to do something about the situation. In his own way, Lou was often quite cynical, but he certainly believed that the Mayor was far more so.

And, of course, there were cries for violence, to answer the violence of Lou's death. One neighborhood newspaper carried the news of the killing, and then editorialized that what was needed was more police, perhaps some extra squads specially trained in guerrilla warfare, to rout and destroy the gangs.

No one realized better than Lou how shrilly inadequate such responses were. He knew that the violence of gang society erupts from the deep frustration of kids who have gone through their whole conscious lives without homes, without fathers, without love, without much of anything. They could hardly have told themselves how much they had suffered, for they had endured by themselves, outside society, without the care of another human being except for the other guys in their gang. And except for Lou, or someone like him, who happened to come along once in a while.

Lou, who had been involved earlier in some of the sit-ins, knew that violence cannot absolve violence, and he knew that the peril to everyone—not just to the gangs—of the police becoming an occupation army in the slum neighborhoods is greater than the danger to him or others in gang warfare.

Besides, Lou knew what it means not to be loved by anybody and what it means not to be loved by everybody.

Lou was a Negro.

He was from a fairly poor family living in the North. He had to save on sleep and work incredibly hard—usually in menial jobs—but because he was intelligent and sensitive, he managed to get a very good education. When I first met him, about five years ago, he was a seminarian at Yale, one of the handful of Negroes who have made it that far. But he grew restless with his studies at Yale; perhaps he felt somehow guilty about being in such a place as Yale Divinity School at all, while his folks were still where they were and while his people were still where they were in this country. For a time, after he left seminary, Lou, in a terrible way, hated the fact that he was a Negro. It was more than feeling sorry for himself; it was as if he complained about his own creation, as if he was rejecting his own birth.

It seemed to him, for a while, better not to live than to be a Negro in America.

After leaving New Haven, he moved to New York City. To act out his resentment, he virtually disassociated himself from bourgeois white society, drifting about the city, unable to look for a job, living on borrowed money, and, it seemed, borrowed time, staying sometimes in flophouses or on the streets.

As he would say himself, he went through the whole bit.

But then, at last, he understood that all this was some variety of pride, that he was indulging in his own self, accusing and condemning himself, punishing and rejecting himself especially for being a Negro; expecting and even, in a way, wanting to be confirmed in this by the rejection of others. Then he realized that he was engaged in suicide.

That was the moment—when Lou was in Hell—in which he knew, I think for the first time, that he was loved by God. That was the event in which by the power of God in the face of the fullness of death, Lou was emancipated —set free to love himself, to love others, and to welcome and receive the love of others. That was the time of Lou's salvation, the time of his reconciliation with himself and with the rest of the world.

What followed was more or less predictable. Having been so intimate with the presence of death in his own life, but having beheld the reality and vitality of the Resurrection in his own life in the same event, Lou was free to live for others.

So that is what he did.

He took this job with the Youth Board and soon was so preoccupied in caring for the kids in his gang that he forgot himself, so fulfilled in his love for others that he lost his self-interest, so confident that he was now secure in God's Word that he was not afraid of death.

He was no longer afraid to die the way he died. He knew about the real risks of his job, especially the way *he* was now free to do his job. The way he died was surely no surprise to Lou. Not that he sought such a death, or any sort of death, any longer, but he was ready to die and was without fear of death. He no longer was in bondage to the alienation of men from each other. He was no longer a pathetic, partisan, professional Negro; he had become a man. Nor was he any longer an imitation white man, a Negro received nominally into white society, as at Yale Lou had been, but never welcomed as himself; he had become a person. Lou himself had been reconciled, and so his own existence and life could be, for the first time, not just a symbol of grievance and protest—as valid and needed in American society as that may be—but more than that, a ministry of reconciliation. He had become so free that he could give away his own life freely—and surely that is the secret of reconciliation in Christ.

Lou Marsh, when he died, was ready; that is, he had already died in Christ and so was without fear of death. That is the freedom the Resurrection bestows upon men.

That is the only way to die, which at the same time means that this is the only way to live.

The Secret of Reconciliation

Part of the witness to reconciliation embodied and enacted in the death of Lou Marsh is the exposure of the fact that racism in any of its forms, among either black men or white men, in American society—and within or outside the churches of American society—is not simply a matter of the presence and power in the public life of the country of certain evil or wicked or aggrandizing or fearful men. Racism is, in its origin, an idol, a principality, one of the works of the power of death in this world: demonic, demanding a service and worship of men, whether white or black, which is radically dehumanizing. Americans, perhaps especially American Protestants, naïvely suppose that racism is a fetish of individuals, a matter of individual prejudice and ignorance. It is that, but much more than that. From the point of view of the Christian faith, the monstrous American heresy is to think that the whole saga of history takes place merely between a celestial God and terrestrial men. But the truth is quite otherwise, both Biblically and empirically: The drama of history takes place among God, men, *and* the principalities and powers, those dominant institutions and ideologies active in this world. It is a shallow humanism which encourages Christians to believe that men are masters of these principalities and powers, including racism. In fact, however, racism has been and still remains for both white men and black men in America the reigning idol which replaces God, and represents that power in the world which is superior to all other powers, save God Himself—the power of death.

This is the power with which Jesus Christ was confronted throughout His own ministry and which—at great and sufficient cost—He overcame. This is the power with which any man who is a Christian has contended and from which—by his own participation in the death in Christ—he is set free. This is the power which must be exposed and openly confronted if there is to be true reconciliation and not simply a modest degree of secular integration of American life.

The issue, at least for Christians—though in the end for every man—is what it means *to be a man.* Much more is involved than legal equality. Much more is at stake than common morality, natural law, or democratic axioms. The issue is not really articulated in the decisions of the courts or enactments of the legislatures, or even in the ideals and goals of the civil rights movements. More —and something different—is required than improved education, better job opportunities, and public integration, if a man is to be a man.

What it means to be a man is to be free from idolatry in any form, including, but not alone, idolatry of race. What it means to be a man is to know that all idolatries are tributes to death, and then to live in freedom from all idolatries. To be a man means to be freed from the worship of death by God's own affirmation of human life in Jesus Christ. To be a man means to accept and participate in God's affirmation of one's own life in Christ. To be a man means the freedom, in the first place, to love yourself in the way in which God Himself has shown that He loves every man.

That is the issue which is most profoundly threatening to both black men and white men at the present time. Their reconciliation one to another first requires that they be reconciled to themselves; to love another means first the freedom to love yourself.

Into that freedom, from time to time, men are baptized. In that freedom men are born into the society of all mankind wrought by God in the life and ministry of Christ. In that freedom is the way and witness of the Cross in which is reconciliation. In that freedom is the love and unity among men which can endure death for the sake of all, even unto a man's own enemy, even unto my own enemy, even unto myself.

*Behold, he is coming with the clouds, and
every eye will see him, every one who
pierced him; and all tribes of the earth
will wail on account of him. Even so.
Amen.*

The Revelation to John 1:7